Aleister Crowley, Frieda, Lady Harris and Betty May

Their Art, Magic & Astrology

ANDREA J. MILES

GREEN MAGIC

Aleister Crowley, Frieda, Lady Harris & Betty May
© 2022 by Andrea J. Miles.
All rights reserved. No part of this book may be used or reproduced in any form without written permission of the Author, except in the case of quotations in articles and reviews.

Green Magic
Seed Factory
Aller
Langport
Somerset
TA10 0QN
England
www.greenmagicpublishing.com

Designed and typeset by CARRIGBOY, Wells, UK
www.carrigboy.co.uk

ISBN 978-1-915580-01-6

GREEN MAGIC

"I've got scars that can't be seen
I've got drama, can't be stolen
Everybody knows me now."

– From the song *Lazarus*, written by David Bowie,
from the album *Blackstar*.

THIS BOOK IS DEDICATED TO

Aleister Crowley, Frieda, Lady Harris and Betty May.

Special thanks you's

Astrodienst for charts generated on *www.astro.com* and used in this book.

Mark Hetherington for photograph and technical support.

Kathy Rowan for enthusiasm and support.

Kevin Rowan Drewitt for astrological knowledge and proof-reading.

To my family and friends for putting up with me through this journey.

The many individuals and organisations that have assisted with particular chapters are acknowledged and thanked at the end of each chapter; there have been many of you and I am deeply appreciative of your help.

Finally, a special thank you to all bohemians, past and present.

Contents

CHAPTER ONE. Aleister Crowley (1875–1947) 8
Ceremonial Magician, Occultist, Novelist, Philosopher
and Poet

CHAPTER TWO. Frieda, Lady Harris (1877–1962) 46
Artist, Illustrator, Student of Magic & Eastern Mysticism
and Suffragist

CHAPTER THREE. Betty May (1894–1980) 99
Dancer, Model and Singer, Clairvoyant and Witch

GLOSSARY OF TERMS 200

CHAPTER ONE

Aleister Crowley (1875–1947)

Ceremonial Magician, Occultist, Novelist, Philosopher and Poet

Aleister Crowley, Ceylon, 1901.
From Wikimedia Commons Public Domain.

EDWARD ALEXANDER CROWLEY (known to many as 'Aleister Crowley') was born into a religious and wealthy family in Leamington Spa, Warwickshire, England on 12th October, 1875. He died at the age of 72 on 1st December, 1947. His father (also called Edward) was born in 1834 and had trained as a civil engineer. However, he never practiced the profession, choosing instead to live as a 'gentleman' up until his death in 1887. He lived on the proceeds of the sale of his shares of the profitable family business, 'Crowley's Alton Alehouses' (Churton, 2012, pp14, 15). Emily Bertha Bishop (1848–1917) was mother to Edward Alexander Crowley. Her family came from Somerset; her father was a dairy farmer and her mother the home keeper. Before her marriage to Edward Crowley in 1874, she had been a governess for a brewer's family (ibid, p17). The marriage produced a son and a daughter: Edward Alexander Crowley and Grace Mary Elizabeth (born in 1880, although sadly their daughter only lived for a few hours).

His father's family had been staunch Quakers, but Edward Crowley Senior rebelled against his religious upbringing, choosing instead to become one of the Plymouth Brethren along with his wife, Emily. They believed that every word in the Bible was divinely inspired and that on the Day of Judgment, only members of their own sect would be saved.

Aleister Crowley dedicated his life to the study and practice of magic, poetry and esotericism and indeed much of his life was devoted to these subjects. He travelled extensively in his geographical and mystical pursuits. During his lifetime he courted controversy and notoriety. As a young man he was educated at Trinity College, Cambridge, where he studied chemistry, English literature and philosophy. He was also a highly skilled chess-player, mountaineer and poet. Crowley was unable to serve his country in the First World War because of phlebitis in his leg. By the time conscription was introduced, he would have been 41 years old, just over the upper limit for conscripts as specified in the Military Service Act of 1916, so he would not have been eligible anyway. He married twice, and had children with both wives.

WHAT ALEISTER CROWLEY'S NATAL CHART SHOWS

Aleister Crowley was born when the Sun was in the artistic and sociable air sign of Libra at 19 degrees and the Moon was in the mystical and sensitive water sign of Pisces at 22 degrees. Astrologer Lois Rodden calculated his time of birth as being at 11:42pm, and *The Confessions of Aleister Crowley* (1989, p35) states that he was born "between eleven and twelve at night."

Crowley's year of birth was very significant to him since he believed he was a reincarnation of the French author and magician Eliphas Levi, who had died that same year (i.e. 1875) (www.controverscial.com). In Crowley's *Magick in Theory and Practice* he discusses his belief that he was the rebirth of Levi, describing 'evidences' as support for the theory of reincarnation.

In Crowley's natal chart there is a special aspect pattern called a Fixed T-Square (*see explanation on right*) and this can be seen in the bottom half of the chart, where it is formed by Saturn, Uranus, and the focal point is Mercury. The tension of this T-Square is released in Taurus at 13 degrees. If one thinks of the T-Square like a drawn bow in tension, then the point where the arrow would be released is (in Crowley's natal chart) opposite Mercury in Taurus at 13 degrees (as noted earlier). The Fixed T-Square pattern suggests that Crowley was born with determination, purpose and willpower. This manifested in his inner strength and ability, enabling him to stand firm when faced with challenges and pressures. Others may even have seen him as inflexible and unyielding, or even a man with a large 'chip on his shoulder.'

> **T-Square**
> A T-Square is a pattern formed when planets in opposition also form a square with another planet. The pattern resembles the letter 'T' when viewed in the chart. The squared planet or point is referred to as the 'focal point'.

In Crowley's natal chart, all the cardinal houses (1, 4, 7 and 10) are occupied by planets. These areas represent the self, including home and domestic life, partnerships and public status, which would have been important to him. The cardinal mode (*see glossary*) in a natal chart indicates an energy which is challenging, initiating and pioneering. There are also a number of hard aspects (oppositions and squares) in Crowley's natal chart. This suggests he would have experienced many challenges and tensions in his life; nonetheless these aspects would have provided him with energy and the determination to succeed.

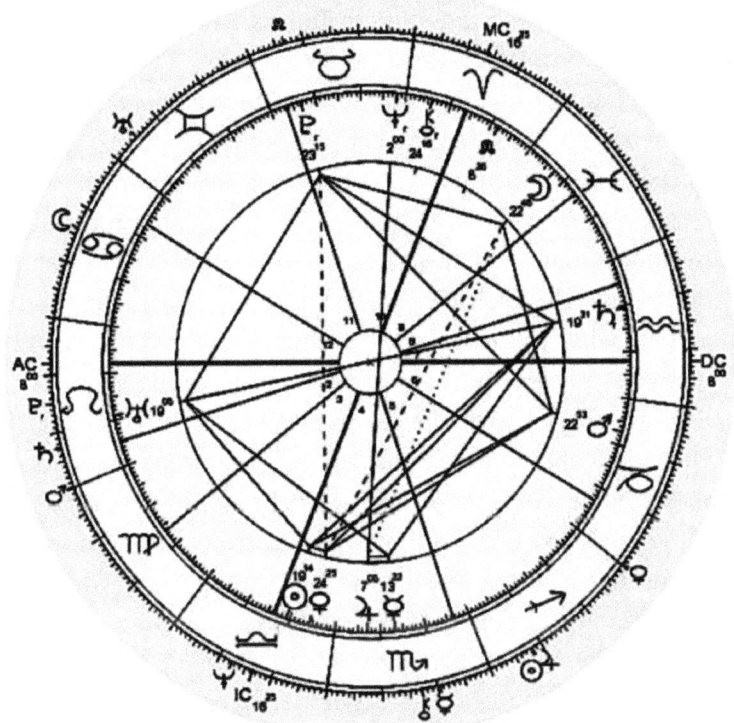

Natal and transits chart for Crowley on the day he died
(1st December, 1947)

The planetary aspects in the chart show a preponderance of square aspects, which are 90 degrees (i.e. three signs apart) and oppositions which are 180 degrees (i.e. six signs apart). Both the square and oppositions are termed 'hard' aspects as they respectively indicate challenges and conflict in one's life. Depending on other themes in an individual's chart, the squares and oppositions can offer the individual the opportunity to accomplish and generate change during their lifetime. The hard aspects in Crowley's chart will be discussed in more depth further on.

The elements in Crowley's chart are well balanced and there is a strong preponderance of the female polarities consisting of: Moon in Pisces, Mercury in Scorpio, Mars in Capricorn, Jupiter in Scorpio, and Neptune and Pluto in Taurus. The female polarities indicate gifts of great artistry, imagination and sensitivity. Crowley certainly channelled these talents and qualities into areas such as painting, writing poetry and ritual magic.

In the natal chart, the sign of Leo is on the ascendant, while Uranus is in Leo in the first house. The ascendant and the first house indicate one's image, persona and approach to the outer world. Leo on the ascendant indicates a sense of the dramatic, combined with theatricality and showmanship. This suggests that Crowley revelled in his creative and distinct appearance.

Leo is associated with performance, and this indicates that he was easily able to direct and lead with a receptive audience. Confidently he could take centre stage when required. One example of this is where he was the centre of attention in the Criminal High Court in 1934 in the 'Black Magic Case' which will be discussed further on in more detail. The Leo ascendant sense of theatricality, can be seen in Crowley's ceremonial magic work when working with the spectators of his group.

FLAMBOYANCE, MONEY AND STYLE

During his time at Cambridge, he wore silk shirts, floppy bow-ties and rings set with semi-precious stones, which give some idea of his flamboyant style and panache. Venus is at home in Crowley's

ALEISTER CROWLEY (1875–1947)

Sun sign, Libra (as Venus is Libra's ruling planet). This would have provided him with an aesthetic talent, including a sense of colour, design, co-ordination and style; all of which added to his unique fashion-sense. Even in his later years, Crowley maintained a very original sense of fashion, with his "... rough tweed jackets and plus-fours, large floppy bow ties, silk shirts and hand-knitted stockings with silver buckles at his knees and on his shoes. Occasionally he held his socks up with silver Tibetan bangles lined with tiny bells" (Booth, 2000, p463). Clearly, he wanted to stand out from the crowd, something in keeping with Uranus in the first house and the Leo ascendant.

Aleister Crowley.
From Wikimedia Commons
Public Domain.

Venus is associated with money, as well as love and beauty, suggesting that Crowley liked to spend his money on artistic and beautiful clothing and objects, which appealed to his refined and sophisticated nature. While he was at Cambridge at least, money was not an issue for him; he was financially secure whilst his parents were alive, and he had received a very substantial inheritance when his father died.

Uranus in the first house adds a sense of extremes and eccentricity where there is a need to be free and unrestrained, whilst making one's mark on the world in an original and unusual way. The individualistic characteristic of Uranus includes deviation, experimentation, noncompliance and shocking. Uranus is detriment in Leo *(see glossary)* bringing a forceful, inflexible and obstinate energy and in its determination a strength which is 'fixed' in nature. However, this position of Uranus in the first house also indicates a capacity to be creative, generous, confident and ingenious.

Being an astrologer himself, Crowley would have been well aware of this, and he once remarked that Uranus possessed "...the faculty of inspiring the most amazing extremes of attraction and repulsion. There is never anything half-hearted about the feeling with which such people are regarded" (Symonds and Grant, 1987, p154). He was clearly aware that having Uranus in the first house could elicit "...a certain antagonism... and he may be described as eccentric or even something stronger" (ibid). This was certainly true of Crowley himself, since he was publicly described by the popular press as 'The Wickedest Man in the World' and a 'Satanist'. He did nothing to dispel that public notoriety, even referring to himself as 'The Great Beast'.

Crowley's Sun sign is in the charming and relationship-orientated Libra, which is ruled by Venus (as previously noted) and the Sun is in 'fall' (*see glossary*) in this sign. In this position, Libra deliberates and can be indecisive, as it constantly strives for balance and harmony as symbolised by its image of 'the Scales'. The Sun is in the fourth house, 10 degrees away from the IC (the area that governs ancestry, home, legacy, roots and parents). The Sun creates some soft and hard aspects to other planets, suggesting he was very much aware of the ego and self.

The Sun's aspects comprise of: Sun conjunct Venus, Sun square Mars, Sun trine Saturn, Sun sextile Uranus, Sun opposite Chiron retrograde and Sun opposite the MC. Interestingly, the Sun, Saturn and Uranus are all at 19 degrees in the natal chart. Therefore, every time a transiting planet had hits at 19 degrees, it would have made aspects to those three aforementioned natal planets in Crowley's natal chart. The planet in transit would then have activated the energies associated with the planet. For example, Mars would energise, Saturn would restrict and Uranus would unsettle them.

ALEISTER CROWLEY (1875–1947)

FRIENDSHIPS, RELATIONSHIPS AND MARRIAGE

The Sun conjunct Venus suggests that Crowley sought to find himself through others and that those relationships were very important to him. Venus is square Mars, suggesting he was very brash and frank about his relationships with both men and women, even though homosexuality was still illegal during his lifetime. It was very risky for Crowley to write erotic literature, such as *White Stains,* which was a book of erotic poetry that included homosexual connotations and was published in 1898 in the Netherlands. Just three years before its publication, the playwright and novelist Oscar Wilde had been convicted of sodomy and gross indecency and sentenced to two years hard labour. Thus, Crowley was taking a huge risk in speaking and writing about his homosexual relationships during such repressive times.

The Venus square Mars aspect suggests that Crowley's assertive side may have been incompatible with his loving side. This is because assertion is connected with Mars, whilst love and affection are associated with Venus. As noted earlier, the square aspects denote challenges and difficulties, hence potential difficulties with his relationships. It is possible therefore that Crowley, being impetuous and reckless in his relationships, often confused lust with love. For example, apparently Crowley visited prostitutes from a young age. He also had affairs while he was still married and had magical relationships with his 'Scarlet Women' (interestingly, Mars governs the colour scarlet/red). The term 'Scarlet Woman' was a term Crowley adopted for a woman with the gift of mediumship and who was in touch directly with the gods. Crowley regarded her as the spiritual companion to The Beast 666, the "mistress of the masters of the universe" (Booth, 2000, p183). Interestingly, both of Crowley's wives (Rose Kelly and Teresa Maria Sanchez) were 'Scarlet Women'; others included the Australian violinist, Leila Wadell (Symonds and

Grant, 1979, p667), and also Pearl Brooksmith who helped look after Crowley in his old age and gave him living expenses. When the latter became ill, however, Crowley seems to have deserted Brooksmith, although he did give her the copyright to his *Simon Iff* stories (Booth, 2000, p453).

The seventh house is associated with significant partnerships, marriage and other one-to-one relationships. The latter would have included Allan Bennett who taught Crowley about magic, and Oscar Eckenstein who taught him mountaineering.

Bennett and Eckenstein were both older than Crowley; Bennett was just three years older whilst Eckenstein was sixteen years Crowley's senior. This is interesting as Saturn, which is associated with older age, is in the seventh house of partnerships. Crowley considered both men authority figures in their fields and respected them immensely. For Crowley's Sun sign Libra, one-to-one relationships would have been important to him, helping him find balance, fairness and steadiness in his life. Bennett's Sun sign was Sagittarius, which would have brought an adventurous and philosophical quality to their relationship; while Eckenstein's was Virgo, bringing a gentleness and kindliness to their relationship.

Another significant and well-known partnership was with Frieda, Lady Harris (the subject of Chapter Two) the artist who painted the images of Crowley's *Egyptian Thoth Tarot* cards, which took them several years to finish (*The Book of Thoth*, Crowley, 1985, biographical note, p12). There is an extra card in the deck, a unicursal hexagram card; whereas most Tarot packs have just 78 cards, Crowley's *Egyptian Thoth Tarot* has 79. Sadly, neither Crowley nor Harris lived to see the deck's publication in 1969, as both had died some years previously – Crowley in 1947 and Harris in 1962. Frieda, Lady Harris met Crowley when she was aged 60 through a mutual friend socialite, Greta Valentine and Crowley considered Harris to be reliable and trustworthy. She became his disciple and he taught her divination in the I-Ching and she eventually became a member of the O.T.O. (*Ordo Templi Orientis*).

ALEISTER CROWLEY (1875-1947)

Originally Crowley had wanted to "execute a pack after the tradition of the Mediaeval editors" (*The Book of Thoth*, 1985, biographical note, p12), and the final result was rich in the imagery of alchemy, magic, astrology and the Qabalah. The lengthy collaboration between Crowley and Harris shows that Crowley was quite capable of maintaining relationships if he wished. Interestingly, Harris was a Sun sign Leo (born 13th August, 1877), so perhaps Crowley with his Leo ascendant recognised her artistic and creative, loyal and noble qualities.

Crowley's own Sun and Venus sign of Libra, suggests he had a romantic nature and probably enjoyed the frills that romance could bring, such as purchasing gifts or wining and dining his partners. However, Libra's indecisive nature indicates that he would find it difficult to choose a partner. The theme of being tested here is illustrated by natal Saturn being positioned in the seventh house – the area of marriage. It is well documented that Crowley had numerous affairs and liaisons. Since Libra is ruled by the element of air, he may have behaved with cool detachment, logic and rationality in his relationships, since these are the characteristics associated with the element of air. This is emphasised further by the planetary seventh house ruler being Uranus in Crowley's natal chart. Uranus is the ruler of Aquarius (another air sign) and Aquarius' nature can be distant and icy, which is in keeping with the coolness of the air element.

Crowley describes his own Sun sign of Libra as: "Air in its most active form, the interpenetrating garment of the globe" (Symonds and Grant, 1987, p51). Saturn is retrograde in Crowley's chart and is in the seventh house of marriage. It could be said that he feared losing his freedom in a one-to-one relationship, such as marriage. Saturn's many associations also include conditions, fear and obstruction. Possibly Crowley overcame his fear of marriage and monogamy by having affairs, sleeping with prostitutes and having one-night stands.

The detached and insubordinate nature of Aquarius possibly helped Crowley to avoid emotional involvement in his relationships. However, the Moon in Pisces may have driven him to romanticise about those relationships, allowing him to escape into fantasy and illusion about the nature of adultery. Uranus in his first house indicates that he could assume a persona of being free and unattached if he so wished.

Crowley had children with each of his wives, and may well have had other children from his many liaisons. Crowley divorced his first wife Rose Kelly as early as 1909 and divorce was unusual in those days. Although he separated from his second wife, he never divorced her. The Aquarian descendant shows that he was drawn to partners who were free-thinking, independent and original. Both his wives chose to marry a man who was already considered infamous, and they in their turn would therefore have been considered just as unconventional in living as single parents after their relationship with Crowley had broken down.

LEADERSHIP, STRENGTH AND WILLPOWER

The Sun square Mars suggests that Crowley was supremely individualistic, preferring to lead rather than follow. He had a vast energy which needed to be channelled and expressed by actively doing something. The square aspect indicates self-assertion which when positively expressed can manifest through areas such as courage and energy with a strong libido and vitality. When negatively expressed, the energy can generate through areas such as impatience, recklessness, impulsiveness and an extreme sex drive. It is not surprising that Crowley enjoyed pursuits such as mountaineering, cliff-climbing and fell-walking and he also enjoyed an active and varied sex life. When he was in his late twenties and early thirties he attempted to climb the whole of the Kangcherijungo Mountain, which is part of the Himalayan mountain range. Although he did not reach the top, he did manage to climb some of the mountain. This particular mountain is recognised as probably the world's most treacherous mountain and shows just how courageous, determined and fearless Crowley really was.

In his natal chart, energetic Mars is trine with intense and determined Pluto, which will have given Crowley a compulsion for winning as well as powers of endurance. While at Cambridge University he was voted President of the Chess Club, believing that playing chess gave one an excellent insight into human psychology (Booth, 2000, p52). Concentration and determination as well as psychology are all associated with Pluto, while ambition and competiveness are associated with Mars, thus demonstrating the aspect of Mars trine Pluto as described previously.

The Sun trine Saturn partile (*see explanation in box on right*) at 19 degrees brings self-sufficiency, self-control and self-discipline as these are areas associated with Saturn. Sun sextile Uranus is partile at 19 degrees and indicates Crowley's innovative, reforming, outrageous, progressive and rebellious nature, since these are areas associated with Uranus. As the sextile is a soft aspect (*see glossary*), it denotes that he did not have to try hard in order to achieve such qualities. He could have easily alienated himself and to some people (including his family, whose Christian piety he rejected) he may have appeared odd or unusual.

> **Partile**:
> An aspect is said to be partile when the objects making the aspect are within one degree of each other. In Crowley's chart, both Saturn and Uranus are at 19 degrees.

The Sun opposite the MC (*see glossary*) in the natal chart suggests that Crowley may have experienced challenges and opposition in his career, especially when his authority was questioned. The MC represents achievement and where one can excel in a career and in Crowley's chart it is in the sign of Aries. Mars is the ruling planet of Aries and is associated with conflict and defiance as well as action, courage, initiation and vigour. Other Mars associations include conquest, lust, passion and sexuality as previously discussed.

In Crowley's natal chart, Mars the ruling planet of Aries is in the sign of Capricorn. We describe its position in Capricorn as in exaltation (*see glossary*) because the forceful nature of Mars is harnessed in Saturn's sign. This placement suggests a need for ambition and success while remaining firmly in control. Mars also represents battle, conflict and fight whilst Capricorn is associated with authority, establishment and society. This is borne out by Crowley wanting to be an authority figure in his work and where he would be taken seriously, yet at the same time he embraced disrepute and notoriety with relish while battling with the establishment.

Mars is in Capricorn in the sixth house the area which governs exercise, health, routine and work and Crowley took these subjects seriously (as befits the nature of Capricorn). Mars in the sixth house would have given him tremendous physical energy and he would have enjoyed being outside with the elements, setting himself challenges and goals.

HEALTH SEX AND VITALITY

Despite Crowley's various ailments throughout his life (such as asthma, bronchitis, depression, gonorrhoea, lesion of the tongue, malaria, phlebitis and syphilis), he was still determined to prove to himself and others how active and vigorous he could be. The Sun is square Mars in his natal chart, indicating tremendous energy and vitality, as previously discussed. The square aspect brings impulsiveness and restlessness, and Crowley would have needed to deal with this in order to release his energy – rock climbing would have provided a perfect solution for this, and indeed he had enjoyed it since childhood. Another physical activity he enjoyed as a child was cycling. This would have allowed him to be not only in control but also to enjoy fresh air and nature.

However, Crowley's vitality with regard to his health was sporadic, and this can be illustrated to some degree by the

ALEISTER CROWLEY (1875–1947)

Sun square Mars aspect. This is because the square represents challenge while the Sun and Mars indicate energy and vigour. Although his natural impulse was to be physically active, his health may have suffered not only due to his over-exertions but because he abused his body and was something of a workaholic.

Depression is associated with Saturn the ruler of Capricorn and this is pertinent to Crowley. In 1899, when Crowley took an alpine vacation with his friend Eckenstein, he wrote *Jezebel and Other Tragic Poems*, publishing the work under the pseudonym of Count Vladimir Svareff. It may have been a way for him to disassociate himself with this work, and perhaps writing poetry was his way of dealing with depressive thoughts at that time.

As an adult, Crowley practiced some aspects of Buddhism and Hinduism, including yoga. This would have enabled him to stretch his skeleton and knees which are parts of the body associated with Capricorn and its ruling planet Saturn. To be effective, yoga must be practiced regularly and supported with a good diet which, along with striving for perfection, are in keeping with the sixth house of the natural zodiac. Crowley recognised yoga's value in avoiding emotions such as anger, fear, lust and greed, etc (Symonds and Grant, 1989, p241). However, Crowley also used sexual practices (tantra) in his yoga, and of course sex is associated with Mars; while control and discipline are associated with Saturn. Teeth are also associated with Capricorn and Saturn. Apparently, Crowley's canine teeth were unusually pointed, although his teeth generally were "stained and going rotten. This may have been aggravated by his long-term dependency on drink and drugs" (Booth, 2000, p458). To make matters worse, when he was in his sixties he fell in a Turkish bath and broke his upper left incisor.

It is well documented that Crowley was bisexual, some of his same sex experiences occurred when he was a younger man and studying at Cambridge. The majority of his heterosexual liaisons were with prostitutes and working-class girls who frequented

Cambridge's pubs, looking for opportunities to sleep with wealthy undergraduates (ibid, p62). Mars (as previously discussed) is associated with lust and sex, something for which he had a great appetite. As Capricorn belongs to the earth element it is possible that he was quite 'earthy' in his sexual activity, possibly his sexual partners may have found him cold, austere and controlling, since these are qualities associated with Capricorn and its ruling planet Saturn. Crowley claimed that going without sex for even 48 hours would "… dull the edge of my mind," showing that he regarded the sexual act as a creative force.

When Mars appears in the sixth house, it is sometimes believed that it indicates sexually-transmitted disorders (Tompkins, 2006, p272). This is certainly borne out when, for example, Crowley contracted gonorrhoea from a Scottish prostitute when he was in his late teens (Churton, 2012, p26) and later caught syphilis when in his second year at Cambridge (Booth, 2000, p61). However, he remained promiscuous, doing nothing apparently to prevent infecting his later partners.

We see Crowley's contempt for the women he slept with not only in his promiscuity, aggression and sadomasochism but in his claim that every male should be "… impregnated with the germ of this virus in order to facilitate the culture of individual genius" (ibid, p62). Interestingly, aggression is associated with Mars, and sadomasochism is associated with Saturn by way of control, deprivation and restriction, which is pertinent to Crowley's Mars in Capricorn (ruled by Saturn) position in his natal chart. Of course, it goes without saying that not every person who has Mars in Capricorn in their natal chart is a sadomasochist!

IMAGE AND SELF-IMAGE

All the planetary aspects created with the Sun (which symbolises the conscious and will) show how Crowley was aware of himself and his identity/identities. For example, when Crowley registered at Trinity College, Cambridge, he originally signed the register as 'Edward Aleister Crowley'. This was a small departure from his birth name but his cousin, Gregor, subsequently persuaded him to drop the first name altogether, and to keep the second name but spell it as Aleister.

Crowley was averse to using his father's name, Edward, as he feared it would be abbreviated to Ned or Ted, "...which had common undertones," and he loathed his family nickname of 'Alick'. He also thought that Alick could be shortened to Alec, which he also felt was 'common' (ibid, p47). This shows how much thought he had given to a new identity before arriving at Cambridge, and also his affectedness about his identity generally. Interestingly, the aspect of the Sun opposing Chiron suggests that Crowley may have been 'wounded' in his quest for individuality. Certainly, that is borne out in his earlier life when his need for recognition as well as being a unique person and rebelling against his upbringing was evident.

Another possibility of the aforementioned aspect is that as Chiron represents the 'wound' in childhood, perhaps Crowley felt he was not at the centre of his parent's world as a child. The Sun is in the fourth house of family and heritage, whilst Chiron is retrograde in the tenth house, both representing family and parents. Although Crowley was an only child (his younger sister lived only a few hours), he may have felt wounded by being sent to boarding schools and colleges, thus creating a distance between him and his parents both physically and emotionally.

Crowley was eleven when his father died, and in astrology the father is symbolised by the Sun. The Sun opposing Chiron aspect could therefore pertain to the wound of grief that he experienced as a child in the deaths of both his sister and his father. After his father's death, Crowley ceased to be an ideal student at school and began misbehaving (Wilson, 1987, p29). Crowley was now released from the limitations and restrictions of his pious Victorian upbringing. He became a free-thinker and nonconformist – both attitudes are associated with the original and unique energies of Uranus, which is found in Crowley's first house (the area which governs the self as discussed earlier).

The 'Wounded Self' Chiron (*see glossary*) in Crowley's natal chart gives some insight to the possibility of fostering various facades and guises. The Sun is the core-self and Chiron is wounded and possibly weeping, so is not at one with the true-self. Crowley gave himself different names and titles throughout his life. Apart from calling himself Aleister while at Cambridge, other names he adopted included The Beast, 666 and The Master Therion. He even self-ennobled by calling himself Sir Aleister Crowley as well as Aleister Crowley Macgregor and the Lord of Boleskine and Abertarff (Booth, 2000, p109). This shows disguise, secrecy and veiling as to who the *real* Aleister Crowley (or rather the *real* Edward Alexander Crowley) was!

THE WIDER WORLD

As previously stated, both the fourth and tenth houses can represent parents in a natal chart. The tenth house also represents one's career and the perception of the public and society towards an individual. It can also indicate authority figures – for example, our parent(s). The outer planets of Neptune and Pluto are in the tenth house in Crowley's chart. As both of those planets are slow moving (and both retrograde), they represent generations of people. Neptune takes approximately 164 years to make a complete cycle, spending approximately twelve years or so in each sign. The eliptical (*see glossary*) nature of Neptune's orbit means that at times it can spend longer in some signs and less in others. Crowley was born when Neptune was in Taurus. Therefore, it could be said that he was born into a generation that became engrossed with art, magic, poetry, religion and creative writing, since the nature of Taurus is 'fixed' and Neptune alludes to the aforementioned subjects.

ALEISTER CROWLEY (1875–1947)

During the 1875–1888 cycle of Neptune in Taurus, it is interesting to note that The Theosophical Society was formally founded in 1875 in New York, U.S.A. and The Blavatsky Lodge of The Society in London was started in 1887 (Lachman, 2014, p245). The Society for Psychical Research was founded in 1882 in England (http://www.spr.ac.uk/), while The Hermetic Order of The Golden Dawn was formed in 1888 with its Isis-Urania temple formed in London (http://www.golden-dawn.aom/eu/). It could be argued that with the Neptune in Taurus position, Neptune's 'magic' and 'spirituality' was being stabilised. This was by way of the visionary ideals of the practitioners, being given security with a 'headquarters' for the aforementioned societies, the ideals being associated with Neptune and the headquarters/home associated with Taurus.

Self-sacrifice is also associated with Crowley's position of Neptune in the tenth house. We see an element of this when he writes in *Confessions* (1989, p582): "I regarded myself as having sacrificed my career and my fortune for initiation." He was for a large part of his life able to adopt that attitude as he was born a wealthy man. However, the cost of several bankruptcies and various law suits meant that late in life he had to rely on generosity of friends and the O.T.O. (Booth, 2000, p457).

Finances and personal assets are associated with earthy and practical Taurus, whilst the unseen, unheard and the vulnerable are associated with Neptune. We can see this in the wider context of English society at that time. For example, the National Society for Protection Against Cruelty to Children (known today as the N.S.P.C.C.) was founded in 1884 by Benjamin Waugh. In 1867, when Neptune was in the pioneering sign of Aries, Thomas Barnardo opened his first home in the East End of London for destitute boys and by 1876 built and developed The Girls Village Home for destitute girls.

During this cycle of Neptune in Taurus, Barnardo and Waugh (who were both affluent and wealthy members of society) channelled their prosperity into charitable works. Pluto in

Taurus shows in a wider context that British society was being transformed, and that there was a compulsion to unearth social taboos, using wealth and status to regenerate areas of society in a very practical and enduring way.

Neptune and Pluto are both outer planets that take a long time to complete a cycle, shown here in the two examples above and how their energies influenced many generations of people over a long period of time. Certainly, during Queen Victoria's reign, society was transformed in many ways, with industrial, scientific and technological advances and Crowley belonged to the generation which was going to experience this transformation.

Considering Pluto in his tenth house of the natal chart, there are indications that Crowley could have pursued a career in psychology, investigation or research, since these areas are associated with Pluto. This influence would have aided Crowley's astrological work and his research in the occult. Persecution is also connected with Pluto and it could be said that society would have wished to persecute him, although it is equally possible that he chose to embrace notoriety as a way of protecting himself. For example, he was known publicly as 'The Wickedest Man in the World' – an epithet that first appeared in a copy of the *John Bull* magazine.

This sensational headline stemmed from the lurid stories that Betty May (a former artist's model and wife of Raoul Loveday the subject of Chapter Three) sold to the press after her husband died at Crowley's Thelema Temple in 1923. She told the press that he died as a result of taking part in a magical ritual, where her husband was forced to drink the blood of a sacrificed cat as part of the ceremony. This was largely what led to many of the sensational and startling headlines about Crowley. Another case in point of such headings came from *The Revue International des Sociétiés Secrètes* which even claimed that "… Crowley drank the blood of children and burned women alive" (Churton, 2012, p315). From these illustrations we can see how he was persecuted in some literature and also by the press.

In 1930, Crowley was invited to lecture at The Poetry Society in Oxford and proposed to speak about the fifteenth century child murderer, Gilles de Rais, who was a practitioner of Black Magic. However, when the local authorities heard about the proposal, they banned the lecture. Being the creative soul that Crowley was, he printed the lecture as a pamphlet, determined not to be beaten (Wilson, 1987, p143).

The position of Pluto in the tenth house can also allude to a fear of being dominated by those in authority, such as a forbidding parent. This fear can be deep-rooted and immovable, since the qualities of Pluto in the sign of Taurus are fixed, irresolute and obstinate. As far as we know, Crowley's parents were not cruel but their outlook, particularly in religious thought, was restrictive, especially for a child who hated constraint (Churton, 2012, p21).

LEGACY AND ROOTS

Neptune in the tenth house provides some insight into the background of Crowley's parents. Amongst other areas, alcohol is just one of the many associations of Neptune. It is interesting that Edward Crowley's family had a lucrative brewing business – Alton Alehouses in Hampshire. The wealth generated from his shares in the family business enabled Edward Crowley Senior to retire even before his son was born. Although as a younger man Crowley senior had trained as a civil engineer, he never practiced it as a profession (as noted earlier). Instead, he went on to pursue his religious activities which included rebelling against the family tradition of Quakerism in favour of the Christian Plymouth Brethren sect, which was founded in Dublin in the late 1820's.

Edward Crowley's unconformity created alienation within his family – a theme which his son would repeat in his own search for a meaningful existence through magic, religion and spirituality. As a young boy, Aleister Crowley had accepted the exclusive Plymouth Brethren as normal, yet at the same time saw it in a detached way (Churton, 2012, p21). Such disconnection is symbolic of Uranus in the first house in his natal chart as that position denotes that the subject can approach the world with detachment and logic rather than sentiment.

Another connection with alcohol and breweries is found with Crowley's mother, Emily, since before she married Edward Crowley she had worked as a governess for a family of brewers. According to Crowley, his mother Emily was also a talented artist (*Crowley Confessions*, 1989, p36), although after her husband died, she struggled with life generally and her religious beliefs in particular. He clearly held his mother in some contempt whereas he had always admired his father (Churton, 2012, p22). The Neptune associations are again shown here, firstly by his mother's artistic talents, and secondly by the distress and sorrow that she experienced. The emotional boundaries between Crowley and his mother may have been further weakened by the geographical distance between them while he was at boarding schools and university.

This theme is also echoed by the Moon in Pisces in his natal chart, where the Moon represents a mother or caretaking figure, whilst Neptune (the ruling planet of Pisces) is associated with martyrdom, sacrifice and vulnerability. Therefore, it could be argued that Crowley saw his mother as a victim in that she made sacrifices, especially regarding her religion; Crowley once said it obliged her to "… perform acts of the most senseless atrocity" (*Confessions*, 1989, p36). He wrote: "the tenth house refers to the mother in a man's horoscope … there is probably a special tendency to religious fanaticism" (Symonds and Grant, 1987, p124). It is possible that he drew upon his own experience of his mother in this observation and interpretation.

ESCAPE AND FREEDOM

Significantly, the Moon is the ruling planet of the twelfth house cusp in Crowley's natal chart, and the twelfth house is the area associated with Neptune and Pisces in the natural zodiac. This indicates a need for retreat, withdrawal, escape and fantasy. The Jupiter opposing Neptune aspect suggests that Crowley longed to escape the mundane and routine of day-to-day life. Indeed he became famous and notorious as a magician, poet and mystic – which is certainly not indicative of a humdrum existence! Jupiter is associated with fame as well as exaggeration, whilst Neptune connects with dreams and illusions. Jupiter is also associated with excess and Neptune with escape (as previously noted), so it could also be said that he longed for 'big escapes' in his life. This is certainly borne out by his continuous exploring overseas and his quest for magic and spirituality. Freedom for Crowley lay in a combination of escape and transcendence – the freedom and independence given by Jupiter and the escapism by Neptune.

Aleister Crowley
(Image under licence from PA Images)

Neptune in the tenth house in Crowley's natal chart also suggests that society may have perceived him as deceitful, as this is also an association of Neptune. He was very much aware of this, emphasising that not only did he try and avoid deceiving others, but wanted to prevent them deceiving themselves (Symonds and Grant, 1979, p582). Accusations of deception would have created tensions with his own need to be idolized, making him easily seduced by the notion of being famous. Above all, he needed a career where he could use his gifts of art, intuition, magic and poetry, since all of these talents correspond with the Neptune. This may have helped him to maintain a healthy balance when experimenting and learning about magic and the ancient mysteries.

The theme of the addict and dependency is also connected with Neptune, particularly in connection with drugs and medicines which Crowley was well known to use. He experimented with a hallucinogenic drug called anhalonium (better known today as Peyote) (Booth, 2000, p285), as well as ether, which he believed to enhance his magic. He also used hashish (ibid, p183) and heroin (upon which he was dependent for many years) (ibid, p357) which shows his high level of addiction and dependency to help create his magic.

Crowley's first novel, published by Collins in 1922, was called *Diary of a Drug Fiend*. It was thought to be based upon Crowley's own drug experiences, reflecting his recreational use of and struggle with drugs. We can see here some of the associations of Neptune, those of: addiction, drugs, escape, transcendence and unreality. These themes are further echoed by the placement of the Moon in Pisces in his natal chart which, as we already know, is the sign ruled by Neptune. The Moon in a natal chart shows how an individual can feel comforted, nourished and satisfied. Crowley's Moon in Pisces therefore indicates that instinctively he felt at home with the Neptunian qualities of healing, illusion, magic and spirituality, as well as those aforementioned areas.

DELUSION AND SELF-CONTAINMENT

The theme of deception is illustrated by several examples in Crowley's life where he bestowed on himself different names and titles. This adds to the sense of fantasy, illusion and mystery which helped to conceal his real self. Perhaps his most famous titles are 'The Beast' and '666'. The title of The Beast was apparently given to him by his mother as a young child when he was misbehaving at home in the company of visitors

> Ironically, as this chapter was being researched and written, news reached the media that Boleskine House had been completely destroyed by fire, leaving no trace of Crowley's former home. In 2022, the Boleskine House Foundation began fundraising to restore the home to its former glory.

(Churton, 2012, p21). Crowley was enthusiastic about this title and clearly believed it fitted his mysterious and rebellious persona. 666 was the number of The Beast in the apocalyptic *Book of Revelations* (Chapter 13, vv15–18) in the New Testament. Crowley had an extensive knowledge of The Bible and so the self-entitlements would have appealed to his outrageous side.

Crowley also used titles such as the Laird of Boleskine and Abertaff, which referred to his house which was called 'Boleskine Lodge' (sometimes known as Boleskine House), situated near an area called Foyers. It was a huge building and Crowley referred to it as a manor house (Booth, 2000, p107). When Crowley bought the property, the papers were signed in the name of 'Aleister MacGregor, of 87 Rue Mozart, Paris.' This was actually the address of Samuel Liddell MacGregor Mathers, one of the founders of the Hermetic Order of the Golden Dawn, a ceremonial magic order (Booth, 2000, p108). Eventually, Crowley shortened this title to 'Lord Boleskine'. For much of his life he referred to himself as 'Sir Aleister Crowley', although there is no evidence that he ever received a knighthood (ibid, p109).

The illusion continued with Crowley giving himself other titles, such as 'Aleister Crowley MacGregor' and sometimes plain 'Aleister MacGregor' (ibid). When he rented a flat in Chancery Lane in Central London, he signed the tenancy agreement in the name of 'Count Vladimir Svareff', in order (he claimed) to observe "... how people treated the upper classes" (ibid, p98).

The 'make-believe' world of Crowley was further embroidered when he took to wearing Highland dress (something Mathers also did), including a kilt of the MacGregor tartan. Like the Lord of a large manor house (Boleskine, although large, had never been a manor), he employed a butler, domestic staff and a gamekeeper. He fished for salmon in the loch and shot grouse and deer in the winter (ibid, p109). From these examples we can see how Crowley indulged in fantasy and romanticism, veiling his true identity in order to create a more congenial one for himself.

HOME HEARTH AND INHERITANCE

In a natal chart, the Moon can also provide useful insight about one's home and domestic environment. Other symbolism of the Moon in Pisces alludes to a home near water as well as a home for sanctuary and retreat. The year 1920 was a hugely significant time in Crowley's life, for he moved abroad with his family and taught in Cefalù. He occupied a small villa, with the intention of using it mostly as a temple and spiritual centre but the place eventually became known as the infamous Abbey of Thelema. The geographical area of the abbey, with its garden full of flowers and fruit was immensely satisfying to Crowley, while the nearby great port and rock of Cefalù meant that Crowley could access the temples of Jupiter and Diana (Wilson, 1987, p119). In his final years, he lived in Hastings, East Sussex, which is close to the sea, while previously he had at one time lived in Richmond, overlooking the River Thames. All these domiciles were near water, and the temple was also a sanctuary and retreat, which is in keeping with the needs and satisfaction of the Moon in Pisces position.

In Crowley's chart, Jupiter is in the fourth house and some of the associations of Jupiter include magnitude and vastness. Therefore, this suggests that Crowley enjoyed large homes, such as the 'manor house' i.e. Boleskine Lodge. He used this lodge for the sole purpose of conducting magic and rituals, although he regularly entertained guests there too. In addition to Boleskine Lodge, there were also domestic premises, a small stone gatehouse called Brown Lodge as well as a boathouse and a coach house. He employed domestic staff, such as a butler and coachman and gatekeeper. This tells us how vast the property was, which is in keeping with the expansive nature of Jupiter.

All in all, his grounds covered 34 acres, which included formal gardens and a large area of lawn, grass paddock, rough moor and woodland (Booth, 2000, p108). He fished in the nearby Loch

Ness and climbed the local mountains. Even before he moved into the property, it had already acquired a reputation amongst the locals for mysterious events, necromancy and strange sightings, so Crowley's arrival simply added to the local apprehension. Jimmy Page, lead guitarist in the band Led Zeppelin (who had a passionate interest in Crowley) bought Boleskine in 1971 and said of it that "strange things happened in that house, which have nothing to do with Crowley. The bad vibes were already there." Page may have been referring to local legend that the house was built on the site of a church which was burned down when the congregation were attending mass, the fire killing them all (*The Scotsman* website – *see bibliography at the end of this chapter*). Curiously, it burned down again in 2015.

At other homes he regularly organised extravagant dinner parties. He took pleasure in throwing curry parties for his dinner guests, deliberately making the curry too hot and spicy and then watching his guests "reactions, describing them as 'ordeal by curry'" (Churton, 2012, p367). However, Crowley enjoyed hot curries and at one time even proposed opening a curry house in London and calling it 'The Black Magic Restaurant', which was especially provocative at that time. Although the project never happened, it was certainly in keeping with his alternative and mischievous way of seeing the world.

Crowley's flat in Chancery Lane, Central London, was also home to magic, ritual and occult study (Booth, 2000, p100). He was in his early twenties when he shared his flat with his friend, Allan Bennett, who was a member of The Society of the Golden Dawn. Crowley allowed Bennett to live with him rent-free in return for teaching him about ceremonial magic. Prior to this, Bennett had been living "by his bootstraps" in the home of Charles Rosher – another student of the occult (ibid). Crowley's offer that Bennett should come and live with him illustrates the compassionate nature illustrated by the Moon in Pisces. The Moon in Pisces and Neptune can also indicate the need to 'save' and 'rescue' others, which is how he may have viewed their arrangement. Certainly, it lasted over a year and they travelled abroad together.

Referring again to Jupiter, it is also associated with foreign, different cultures and long-distance travel and, as previously discussed, it is positioned in the fourth house of Crowley's natal chart. This is an indication that Crowley may have had homes overseas. Crowley did indeed live abroad, often doing so whilst on his magical and spiritual adventures. Jupiter is also connected with teaching and preaching and this is certainly borne out in his heritage and upbringing, relating to his father's preaching of his Plymouth Brethren beliefs.

Often considered a beneficiary planet (*see glossary*), Jupiter indicates that Crowley gained riches and wealth through inheritances and legacies. This is because Jupiter is positioned in Scorpio in his natal chart and is the sign associated with death and transformation. Crowley inherited a vast amount of money when he was 21 from his father's legacy, which made him financially secure for much of his life. The money also allowed him to spend much of his life practicing and studying magic whilst travelling abroad, although eventually he succeeded in spending it all and ran up sizable debts through lawsuits and a certain lifestyle.

Although Crowley had never really had to worry about 'going without' when he was at boarding school, he always believed he was kept short of money because his parents feared he would spend irresponsibly on books, tobacco, theatre and women. He blamed them for his lack of financial responsibility in later life (Booth, 2000, p45).

Jupiter in Scorpio reveals Crowley's need to be emotionally moved with what he believed in and that he had a tremendous faith (an attribute of Jupiter). He also had a driving and almost obsessive interest in matters pertaining to life after death as well as research, the occult and sex. All of these subjects are associated with Scorpio and its ruler Pluto. Crowley's attitude and views towards sex were very much at odds with the Church and society at the time.

AUDIENCE, HUMOUR AND WIT

Mercury represents humour and wit in astrology and is also the planet associated with communication, intelligence and speech. In Crowley's natal chart, Mercury is positioned in Scorpio. This indicates that he had a skill in 'dark one-liners.' This is because the nature of Scorpio is intense and able to get to the heart of the matter in few words. However, it also shows that Crowley could be hurtful and spiteful, since these are some of the negative qualities associated with Scorpio and its ruler Pluto.

Mercury also creates aspects with other planets in his natal chart which comprises of; Mercury conjunct Jupiter, Mercury square Saturn, and Mercury square Uranus. Mercury conjunct Jupiter suggests that Crowley enjoyed merriment, 'clowning around' and also pomposity, which are all attributes of Jupiter. The aforementioned aspect also suggests that Crowley was broad-minded, since Jupiter is associated with width and Mercury with the mind. The square aspect between Mercury and Saturn indicates that Crowley's humour could be presented with a straight face and good comic timing – areas that are associated with the dry and sombre nature of Saturn.

Mercury square Uranus suggests that Crowley's humour could also be outrageous and shocking, in keeping with the nature of Uranus. For example, once, after an argument, his mistress Hanni had grown weary of Crowley's dramatic acts of sexual magic with her and she decided to leave him at the hotel where they had been staying. Crowley pretended to commit suicide, leaving a suicide letter underneath his cigarette case at the hotel where they were staying. He then pursued Hanni to her home in Germany, leaving the press to speculate about his supposed 'suicide' (Wilson, 1987, p144).

Crowley's wit has been described as "prodigious, very quick, sharp and caustic" (Booth, 2000, p464). Once, when a lady friend asked him which was the best ladies' college for her daughters to attend, he suggested Radcliffe Hall. This, very Saturnian reply was a play on words as Radcliffe Hall was in fact the name of a famous lesbian author who wrote the book *The Well of Loneliness* and not a hall in the sense of a college (ibid). There are hard aspects created to the Leo ascendant comprising of Mercury square the ascendant, Jupiter square the ascendant, and Neptune square the ascendant. This suggests that Crowley often went 'over the top' in his communication, delivery and expression, whilst at the same time often being offended himself and very sensitive to criticism. He may have used humour to help conceal his authentic self, since Scorpio and its ruler Pluto work to conceal and veil. This would have provided him with a mask and platform for his public persona. We see the importance of humour in Crowley's philosophical work in his remark: "The common defect of all mystical systems previous of the Aeon whose Law is Thelema is that there has been no place for laughter" (http://ac2012.com).

PASSIONATE MESSENGER OF MYSTERIES AND PHILOSOPHY

Mercury in Scorpio indicates a perceptive and intuitive mind with tremendous mental stamina and an interest in what motivates people. This placement also suggests an aptitude for detective work, investigations and research. It is unsurprising, therefore, to know that Crowley apparently became involved with areas such as spying, espionage and the secret service, areas which are all associated with Scorpio and Pluto. Throughout the early twentieth century, he was 'of interest' to Scotland Yard and M.I.6. – the Secret Intelligence Service otherwise known as the S.I.S. (Churton, 2012, p315). Ian Fleming, the well-known author of the *James Bond* novels, was also a wartime Navy Intelligence Officer with the Royal Navy Volunteers and knew Crowley. Fleming toyed with the idea of using Crowley to feed misinformation to the Nazis through Rudolph Hess. However, Fleming's senior, Vice-Admiral John Godfrey, Director of Naval Intelligence, rejected Crowley's offer to interview Hess who then was imprisoned on a country estate called Trent Park in North London (Booth, 2000, pp471–472). There is some conjecture that Hess' capture by the allies was due to Crowley's psychic efforts. Although, given his fondness for self-aggrandisement, it may just have been a rumour that Crowley put about to enhance his own status. There was also a persistent rumour that Crowley participated in one ritual held in Ashdown Forest as part of the psychic warfare against the Nazis (Booth, 2000, p472). It must be said though that several other psychics and witches (including Cecil Williamson, founder of the Museum of Witchcraft) also made the same claim.

Mercury conjunct Jupiter would have helped in Crowley's research and writing. Mercury is associated with reading and writing and Jupiter is connected with publishing. It is interesting, therefore, that Crowley often self-published his own writing. This may have been because some publishers did not want to risk being associated with Crowley and his notorious reputation.

Since Jupiter is also associated with philosophy, it is not surprising that Crowley developed his own philosophy called Thelema, of which ritual magic is a key principle of the philosophy. The other belief and ethical code of the Thelemites was (and still is): "Do What Thou Wilt Shall Be The Whole Of The Law" – which essentially means that "every individual has a right to autonomy, to develop as he sees fit, to find a way of life compatible with his most basic wishes and true will, but in harmony with his surroundings" (Booth, 2000, p186).

Mars is creating a trine aspect with Pluto, indicating an interest in magic and the occult, and therefore many forms of hidden power will have appealed to Crowley. Mars is in the sixth house, the area of health and work; while Pluto is in the tenth, which is the area of career and society. This reveals that Crowley was successful and at ease with his magical work and the occult and was able to make a career out of it by careful application of his strong willpower and self-expression.

In Crowley's chart, the Moon is in the ninth house, which is the area that in the natural zodiac governs Sagittarius and Jupiter. This is associated with adventures, beliefs, higher education, long-distance travel, religion, philosophy, vision and publishing. Certainly he had many adventures abroad visiting countries such as America, Ceylon, China, Egypt, Colombo, India, Mexico, Morocco, Russia, Sicily and Tunisia. It is probable that he would have felt comfortable and at home wherever he travelled. This is because the Moon in the ninth house shows that he felt a sense of satisfaction and security in adventuring and exploring in foreign lands. Given the energy of the Moon is shifting, this would have helped him adapt and adjust; embracing the history, customs and heritage of the places he was visiting.

Returning to the Higher Education association of the ninth house and Jupiter, it was certainly significant in Crowley's life as was his earlier education. He went to Cambridge University and while there changed his course from Political Economy to English Literature (Booth, 2000, p49). Earlier on and from the age of eight, Crowley had been educated at various educational establishments, having had home tutors in his earlier life. School had been a horrible experience and he experienced bullying, punishment and sexual violation by teachers and fellow students alike during that period which left him experiencing bouts of depression (Booth, 2000, pp32–33). Overall, his education was unsettled as he changed school several times due to bullying.

Pain and suffering are both associated with Crowley's Moon sign of Pisces and its ruler Neptune, and the aforementioned experiences may have helped to shape his feelings towards others in positions of helplessness, as in the example of his friend, Alan Bennett, who was discussed earlier on.

ALEISTER CROWLEY (1875–1947)

SORROW, STAMINA AND SURVIVAL

The Moon is sextile Pluto in Crowley's natal chart, suggesting that Crowley had tremendous ability and inner strength to process crisis, pain and tragedy – and intense themes of survival and transformation were significant in his life. From early childhood, Crowley experienced trauma, at school and also with the death of his father and that of his newborn sister. Death (both metaphorical and physical) is an associate of Pluto and Crowley admitted later in his life that he possessed "... a strain of congenital masochism" (Booth, 2000, p12). The Moon is emotional and sensitive while Pluto is intuitive and insightful, so it is likely that Crowley early on developed a 'survival kit', in that his feelings (Moon) were sensitive to any acts of betrayal, sabotage and treachery (associations of Pluto) where confidentiality and trust may have been broken.

The themes of 'hard lessons to learn' are indicated in Crowley's chart whereby Mercury is square Saturn, so the lessons are indicated by Mercury and hardship by Saturn. Mercury associates with schooling and Saturn discipline. Through this we can see evidence of a strict schooling, which was evident in the harsh environment that Crowley found himself in at various boarding schools, such as White Rock Boarding School for Young Gentlemen and Malvern College. However, discipline can be very helpful in some circumstances, especially if applied fairly; such order and control may have been helpful to Crowley when he was writing.

As Mercury is also associated with knowledge, whilst Saturn is an authority figure and taskmaster, it could be said that Crowley mastered an area of knowledge and expertise. Mercury is in Scorpio, indicating that he had knowledge and interest in life's mysteries which included: magical knowledge, the occult, sex and sex magic. These are all areas associated with Scorpio and its ruler Pluto. Saturn is in Aquarius which suggests that, as in

Crowley's case, life is about pursuing an alternative lifestyle where the unusual and unconventional were essential.

Mercury square Saturn can also indicate a lack of books in the home, since Mercury associates with information, knowledge and reading, whilst Saturn represents restriction and deprivation. This interpretation is borne out when, as a child, Crowley claimed he only had access to The Bible, a few religious texts and a history of the Indian mutiny, which were filled with Christian values and morals (Booth, 2000, p12). Unsurprisingly, Crowley had a tremendous knowledge of the scriptures and from an early age was fascinated by stories involving The Beast with the number 666, The False Prophet and The Scarlet Woman. These themes later proved to be hugely significant in his magical work, both practical and written.

Another interpretation of the aspect Mercury square Saturn is that relating to the death of a sibling, which was pertinent in Crowley's life. This is because Saturn represents the end of a cycle and death and decay, while Mercury indicates one's siblings. As previously mentioned, Crowley's mother gave birth to a daughter who lived for only a few hours. In the book, *Confessions* (Symonds and Grant, 1989, p42), Crowley describes being taken to see his dead baby sister, although he was only four years old. Writing with the knowledge of adult hindsight, he remarked that he did not "… see why he should be disturbed so uselessly. He couldn't do any good; the child was dead; it was none of his businesses."

Whether this is how he had really felt as a child, or as a man looking back on the event is difficult to say. The dead sister, Grace Mary Elizabeth was born on February 29th, 1880, making her a Sun sign Pisces, the same sign that was Crowley's Moon sign. Had she lived, the two of them may well have experienced an understanding and intuitive brother and sister relationship. Crowley's natal chart indicates a natural strength of self-sufficiency indicated by the Sun trine Saturn. This and the above-mentioned aspect of Mercury square Saturn could have helped

Crowley to learn from his mistakes, albeit over a very long period of time, since the nature of Saturn is slow and persevering.

Crowley was anarchic and very much ahead of the Victorian times and the class into which he was born. He had a wealth of knowledge about ancient truths and magical systems and built upon this. He used his determination to grow and perfect that knowledge. Although he could be charming, witty and creative, his powerful intellect did not permit him to suffer fools gladly, especially those who were less spiritually aware than himself. Nevertheless, he had a wide circle of acquaintances and friends. In the wider public domain (especially in the popular press) he was portrayed as an evil black magician, a drug addict and wicked sexual deviant. Yet he seems to have enthusiastically embraced this disrepute and notoriety. During his lifetime, Crowley's philosophy and work was ridiculed by society (although not in the bohemian circles in which he moved). His beliefs and magical work seemed to have been more accepted and welcomed in the late twentieth century.

Crowley died at the age of 72 from chronic bronchitis and myocardial degeneration (deterioration or inflammation of the heart muscle). In his life, he had suffered with malaria, phlebitis, lesion of the tongue, gonorrhoea and asthma. He died on the 1st December, 1947, and during this time he was experiencing some 'hard' transits. Transiting Pluto was in the first house and was square natal Mercury. Pluto is the planet of death and transformation while Mercury is the planet of communication and health. It symbolises an intense time where deep thinking, new ideas and philosophies would have taken on an even deeper meaning for him. It can also suggest significant change in health and well-being. There may be insight, that knowledge is power and to a degree this does show up in his final years, Crowley lived in a retirement home in Hastings called Netherwood and although he was physically ill, he was mentally still very active and productive. During his time here, he continued his great

Aleister Crowley.
From Wikimedia Commons
Public Domain.

work of formulating his magical philosophy, Thelema. His friend, occultist Kenneth Grant, acted as secretary to him and Crowley dictated letters, produced charters for magical lodges and continued to receive guests, including his loyal friend and painter of his Tarot cards, Frieda Harris; she even painted him shortly before he died, as was his wish. As transiting Pluto was in the first house (the area which governs the self), it reveals that Crowley was more controlling and intense than previously (such are the qualities associated with Pluto) and he may have been more compulsive and obsessive in his communications and ideas. He may also have been darker and broodier and perhaps experienced more mental pressure than before.

The inevitability of death probably inspired Crowley to complete his final work and in his thinking he was determined to complete his mission. The metaphysical death of Pluto can be seen in the resurrection of his work, it being more appreciated after his death by future generations.

Transiting Saturn in the first house was square natal Pluto in Crowley's chart. Saturn transits ask us to remove that which is now unnecessary in our lives, both in terms of materialistic possessions and values. The square aspect brings challenges, frustrations and tensions. Therefore, transiting Saturn square natal Pluto suggests it was inevitable at this time that Crowley was being forced to overhaul his life. Both Saturn and Pluto are planets that are associated with beginnings and endings and the completion of cycles.

ALEISTER CROWLEY (1875–1947)

Transiting Uranus in the eleventh house was square the natal Moon, Uranus transits bring breakaways and restlessness. The eleventh house represents friends and long-term goals and visions, while the Moon indicates our emotions and domestic life. It could be said that Crowley experienced unsettling emotions at this time; he may have felt that his emotional freedom was being challenged and curtailed too, whilst some friends may have become less dependable. This transit may have helped him to assist others by nurturing new generations of magicians and philosophers through his published work.

On the day that Crowley died, his Sun and Venus (Libra) had progressed into Capricorn as had Mercury. Saturn (the ruler of Capricorn) is associated with diligence and longevity. Certainly, it would appear that he became far more respected and valued posthumously by later generations.

Crowley's influence has been undeniably widespread. For example, his picture can be seen on the cover of The Beatles' *Sgt Pepper's Lonely Hearts Club Band* album. Singer Ozzy Osborne with two of his guitarists penned a song called *Mr Crowley*. David Bowie sang about Crowley in the song *Quicksand*, with the lyrics: "I'm closer to the Golden Dawn, immersed in Crowley's uniform of imagery." The 2008 film release of *Chemical Wedding* (co-written by and featuring Bruce Dickinson of the heavy metal band Iron Maiden) features a Cambridge scholar being possessed by the spirit of Crowley, played by the actor Simon Callow. The late Brian Jones, founder of The Rolling Stones, was said to be fascinated with Aleister Crowley and that his fascination with the occult was "… a cover story for his sexual experimentation" (Trynka, 2014, p181). This shows that Crowley's enduring legacy crossed generations into the twenty-first century.

Crowley's message for humankind, "Do What Thou Wilt," was evident in his own life of mysticism, physical and spiritual explorations. It is significant that Crowley wrote the *Book of Thoth*, in which Thoth came to educate the Egyptians and taught them to read and write. Crowley in his lifetime educated others about ancient truths, ceremonial magic and hidden knowledge.

Edward Alexander Crowley left a significant legacy to the world. He had a brilliant, innovative mind, coupled with great purpose and willpower. He regarded himself as a prophet with a message of sincerity, which was to help lead humankind into an advanced and progressive twentieth century, then individuals could be true to themselves and realise the self through magical and religious expression.

ACKNOWLEDGEMENTS, CREDITS & REFERENCES

Chart generated by www.astro.com

Birth data: Crowley, Aleister: Tuesday 12th October, 1875, 23:42pm, GMT, Royal Leamington Spa, England, U.K. 1w31,52n18.

Source: Symonds and Grant, 1989, state that Crowley was born between 11:00pm and midnight.

Rodden Rating: 'C' Collector Rodden, source of data: rectified from approximate time.

Harris' Birth Certificate (Birth Certificate, General Register Office, No. BXCG 672416).

BOOKS

Booth, M. (2000) *A Magick Life: A Biography of Aleister Crowley*. Coronet Books.

Churton, T. (2012) *Aleister Crowley: The Biography*. Watkins Publishing.

Crowley, A. (1985) *The Book of Thoth, by The Master Therion (Aleister Crowley)*. Samuel Weiser Inc.

Lachman, G. (2004) *Aleister Crowley: Magick, Rock n Roll and the Wickedest Man in the World.* Tarcher.

Symonds, S. and Grant, K. (Eds.) (1987) *Aleister Crowley: The Complete Astrological Writings.* W.H. Allen & Co. Plc.

Symonds, J, and Grant, K. (Eds.) (1979) *The Confessions of Aleister Crowley: An Autohagiography.* Arkana Penguin Books.

Tompkins, S. (2006) *The Contemporary Astrologer's Handbook.* Flare Publications in conjunction with the London School of Astrology.

Trynka, P. (2014) *Sympathy for the Devil.* Transworld.

Wilson, C. (1987) *Aleister Crowley: The Nature of the Beast.* The Aquarian Press.

WEBSITES

http://ac2012.com/2012/08/05/aleister-crowley-myths-actually-true/ – Accessed on 27/11/2015.

http://www.barnardos.org.uk/what_we_do/our_history/thomas_barnardo.htm – Accessed October, 2015.

http://www.golden-dawn.aom/eu/displaycontent.aspx?pageid=71 – Accessed October, 2015.

https://www.nspcc.org.uk/fighting-for-childhood/about-us/organisation-structure/ – Accessed October, 2015.

http://www.spr.ac.uk/page/history-society-psychical-research-parapsychology – Accessed October, 2015.

http://www.thelemapedia.org/index.php/Sex_magick – Accessed on 22/11/2015.

https://en.wikipedia.org/wiki/Charles_Henry_Allan_Bennett – Accessed on 28/11/2015.

https://en.wikipedia.org/wiki/Oscar_Eckenstein – Accessed on 28/11/2015.

http://www.controverscial.com – Accessed on 02/09/2015.

http://www.thelemapedia.org/index.php/Eliphas_Levi – Accessed on 02/09/2015.

http://www.scotsman.com/lifestyle/culture/music/aleister-crowley-s-inverness-mansion-destroyed-by-fire-1-3983595 – Accessed on 15/01/2015.

CHAPTER TWO

Frieda, Lady Harris (1877–1962)

Artist, Illustrator, Student of Magic & Eastern Mysticism, Suffragette

Frieda Harris.
Photo Courtesy of Paul Ashford Harris (Grandson of Frieda, Lady Harris)

FRIEDA HARRIS was born Marguerite Frieda Bloxam on 13th August, 1877 in Pimlico, England. She was daughter to John and Jessie Bloxam. Her father, John Astley Bloxam, was

FRIEDA, LADY HARRIS (1877-1962)

a successful surgeon who made significant contributions to the medical profession. Her mother, Jessie Findlay (née Porter), was an active suffragist. Frieda was the middle child of three children; she had an elder sister, Florence Mary (who married a doctor in South Africa), and a ten-year-younger brother, Owen Astley (who became an architect). Frieda went to art school (date unknown) – something she was determined to do from a young age. Later, she married Percy Harris. He became a prominent Liberal M.P. for Bethnal Green, East London and represented a strong working-class area. He became Liberal Chief Whip and Deputy Leader of the Liberal Parliamentary Party. He then became Sir Percy Harris, first Baronet, in 1932 and Frieda rightfully took the title of Lady Harris. She showed her independence by wanting to be known as Frieda, Lady Harris to indicate that she was a person in her own right and not just an appendage to her husband. Technically speaking, she was only entitled to call herself *Lady Frieda Harris* if she had been born (for example) to a duke and then permitted to use a courtesy title through her father (DuQuette, 2017, p14). Sir Percy Harris and Lady Harris had two sons together; Jack was born in 1906 and Thomas Nicholas in 1908.

Percy Harris.
From Wikimedia Commons, Public Domain.

Frieda was passionate about art, supported the women's suffragist movement and was a member of the non-militant National Union of Women's Suffrage Societies (N.U.W.S.S.). Harris was also a collaborator and a very loyal friend to author and ceremonial magician, Aleister Crowley. She became famous in occult circles for painting the brilliant images of the *Thoth Tarot* deck which was designed by Crowley. The deck underlines his

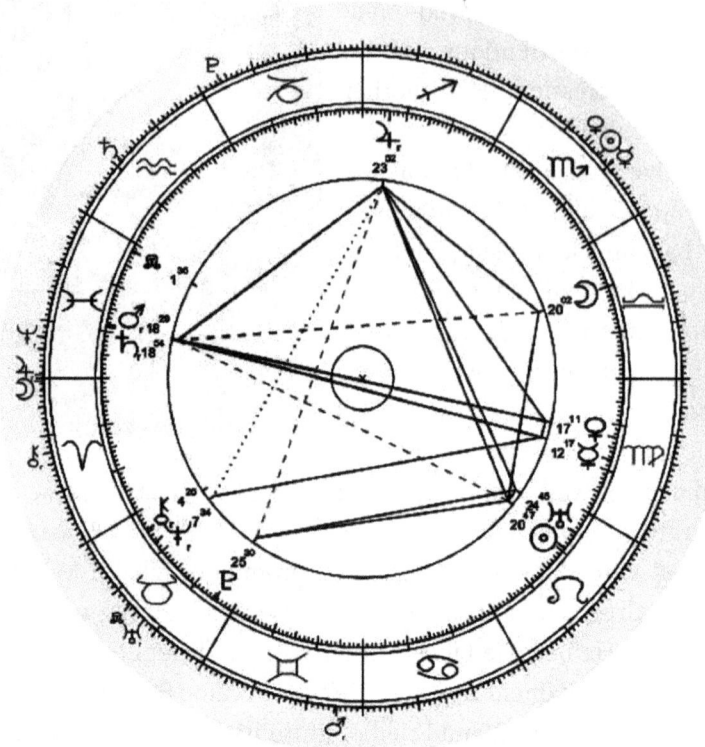

Marguerite Frieda Harris' natal chart and the transits to it on the day she died, 5th November, 1962

book, *The Book of Thoth*, and today the deck remains extremely popular. Harris was a Co-Mason and also a member of the mystical orders Argenteum Astrum and the Ordo Templi Orientis, which she had been introduced to by Crowley. Her magical name, whilst in the latter order, was Sister Tzaba (which means 'Hosts'). Harris was utterly committed to Crowley and the Tarot project upon which they collaborated (which lasted several years) and even after his death, she continued with passion to ensure that a publishing contract for a general release for both the *Thoth Tarot* deck and *The Book of Thoth* was reached.

Harris also illustrated books, wrote poetry, designed book covers and exhibited her paintings at places such as the New

English Art Club and the Berkeley Galleries. As well as that, she designed stage sets. After her husband died in 1952, she emigrated to India to pursue her spiritual quest; she remained there until she died in Srinagar, Kashmir in 1962 on 5th November.

WHAT FRIEDA HARRIS' NATAL CHART SHOWS

Marguerite Frieda Harris was born on the 13th August, 1877, when the Sun was positioned at 20 degrees in Leo and the Moon was in Libra. As her time of birth is unknown, one cannot be certain of the exact degree of the Moon's position in Libra, therefore we do not know for certain the ascendant sign and house cusps in her natal chart.

In her birth chart she had a preponderance of planets in the earth signs comprising of; Mercury and Venus in Virgo as well as Neptune and Pluto in Taurus. This indicates that she had a practical, organised and productive disposition. Each of the aforementioned planetary positions will be discussed further on in detail. There is also a distinct presence of the fire element in her natal chart which comprises of; Sun and Uranus in Leo, and Jupiter in Sagittarius. This suggests that, Harris was optimistic and independent, as well as philosophical in her outlook; these positions will also be discussed further on in more detail.

There is a mutable T-Square (*see glossary*) in her natal chart with a focus point of 23 degrees in Gemini. This configuration involves planets which are in signs governed by the mutable mode (*see glossary*) which are: Mercury and Venus in Virgo, Mars and Saturn in Pisces, and Jupiter in Sagittarius. These particular signs of the zodiac are restless in energy but can also be flexible and versatile, although the mutability can also generate irritability and tetchiness. However, this type of energy would have also helped her to be less adamant and obstinate, which are some of the characteristics associated with the fixed (*see glossary*) signs in her natal chart. The planets in the fixed signs of her natal chart are; Sun and Uranus in Leo, and Neptune and Pluto in Taurus and will be discussed further on.

The focus point of the T-Square reveals where there may have been tensions in her life and as the focus point is in Gemini, the areas which may have been challenging include siblings and neighbours, as well as communication and education. We can see some contention post her early education. Harris was sent to a small private establishment in Broadstairs, Kent; there she was taught by a woman who had trained to be an artist, a Miss Osmond (www.brill.com/Aries/Whitehouse 2021, p127). When Harris left school, she had an above-average standard of French and had already started to paint but her lack of academic schooling "haunted her throughout her life" (ibid). In August of 1940, a communication between Harris and Aleister Crowley talks about her early education, acknowledging that there was "neither Latin or Greek … no classical education, indeed no education" (www.brill.com/Aries/Whitehouse 2021, p132).

The dominant polarity in her natal chart is the feminine one, which means that the earth and water signs are more prevalent, showing an artistic, imaginative and intuitive nature. Two planetary positions which are significant in her natal chart are Mercury in Virgo and Jupiter in Sagittarius. This is because the planets are in the sign which they rule, which means the planets are able to work at their optimum level in these signs. Interpretations for the planetary positions will be provided later. The hard aspects in her natal chart suggest that she faced many challenges and conflicts in her life. However, through her aptitude and determination we will see further on how she was able to achieve much in her life. Harris has four planets which are retrograde (*see glossary*) in her natal chart; just twelve per cent of the population have four planets retrograde in their natal chart (www.twixtearthandsky.com) which in itself makes her quite a unique human being. The retrograde planets in her chart are:

Mars, Jupiter, Saturn and Neptune and the asteroid Chiron is also retrograde.

CREATIVITY AND SOCIABILITY

Her Sun sign Leo shows that at heart she was creative and playful, generous and optimistic, loyal and hospitable. Her Moon sign Libra shows she could be charming and kind. She would have enjoyed socialising and intellectual stimulation too. Certainly she would have had this experience when she regularly dined with Aleister Crowley as they discussed their project of creating the *Thoth Tarot* deck. Examples of the restaurants where they dined include Queens Restaurant in Sloane Square and Bentley's Oyster Bar and Grill in St. James (Churton, 2021, pp81,95). Harris also had an appreciation of the arts; a sense of the aesthetic and also beauty. These are all areas associated with Venus the ruler of her Moon sign Libra (Venus also rules Taurus). She was known, for example, to frequently entertain and host parties at her homes in London. "She entertained, often with costume parties, the literary, artistic and theatrical glitterati of the day" (Booth, 2000, p473).

On one occasion, "An unexpected caller to Harris' home stood outside and heard piano music and the sweet tones of Debussy's *'Clair de Lune'* ... when the front door was opened, it was evident a party was in progress and a pianist was entertaining guests" (https://rwwgroupblog.com). Her eldest son Jack recalled that, "When she was first married, she was very social and did a lot of entertaining at her house in Sloane Square" (https://visualmelt.com *Memoirs of a Century*).

This shows the enjoyment and warmth that she had for other people and how she wanted to ensure they had a cordial time when she was playing hostess. This is very much in keeping with her hospitable Leo nature; she has been described as: "A well-known eccentric society hostess" (Booth, 2000, p473). Being appreciated and holding court, as well as taking pleasure in seeing people enjoy themselves, is very much in keeping with the Sun Leo and Moon Libra characteristics.

Harris also socialised by meeting friends in clubs which existed for those in 'high society'. For example, she regularly frequented the Sesame and Pioneer Club, enjoying drinks and lunch with critic and poet, Dame Edith Sitwell (Ashford Harris, 2018, p19). She and Aleister Crowley were both friends of artist and bohemian, Greta Valentine (http://www.artsmarket.co.uk), and the two women dined at the Café Royal together, as well as at The Royal Automobile Club (Bax, 1951, p54). Harris also had a great friendship with the actress Dame Edith Evans (Ashford Harris, 2018, p228); no doubt Harris experienced a meeting of minds with such artistic and intelligent women and would not have been short of conversation.

She also became friends with the famous Indian choreographer and classical dancer, Ram Gopal, who described her as being "my dear friend" (Gopal, 1957, p196). This description of Harris was given by him when she was in India. She helped him during a time when he was "disconsolate" (ibid), his nerves in a state of array as he was experiencing financial problems with his ballet production. She suggested that they go to the Taj Mahal "and speak to the spirit of Shah Jehan and Mumtaz Mahal and tell them, ask them to help us" (ibid).

The ballet was successful so clearly their prayers were answered! Gopal had a huge influence on Harris, which in part led her to emigrate to India. It has been said that she was infatuated with Gopal and she financially assisted him and followed him out to Ceylon (modern-day Sri Lanka). There he was making a Hollywood film, *The Elephant Walk*, (Ashford Harris, 2018, p197) and was employed as choreographer for the film (https://www.imdb.com). The film was released in 1954 and starred Elizabeth Taylor, Dana Andrews and Peter Finch.

It was through Gopal that she met the famous Sinhalese painter and poet, George Keyt. She said of him: "His paintings are easily the equal of Picasso in vigour, and much deeper in emotion" (Ashford Harris, 2018, p257). Keyt taught her much about the Lord Buddha and Hindu gods, which must have appealed to her curiosity about different religions and spirituality. Clearly, Harris enjoyed socialising with artistic and creative people and would go to great lengths to be around kindred spirits.

Ram Gopal.
Wikimedia Commons Public Domain.
Author: Carl Van Vechlen, Library of Congress Catalogue.

DISTINCTION, INDEPENDENCE AND LIBERTY

The Sun is conjunct Uranus in her natal chart (as previously noted) and this suggests that freedom and independence were important to Harris. At times she may have been construed by other people to be radical and unorthodox. Uranus is also associated with: idealism, humanity and truths and another association of Uranus is being involved in groups/kindred spirits and their activities.

It is possible that part of Harris' strong wilful independent nature may have started to develop in her early years. For example, the 1891 Census shows that she was a student at a boarding school; Valetta House in Broadstairs, Kent. This shows that from a young age a distance and detachment (associations of Uranus) were created between her and her parents. This was because she was nurtured by professionals, i.e. teachers in boarding school. In doing so, she must have harnessed a degree of self-sufficiency and learnt not to rely on her parents for comfort and emotional support. It is possible that Harris also developed her inner strength and autonomy from this young age. This would have helped to make her the determined and strong-willed person that she was. It also illustrates one example of the Sun conjunct Uranus aspect at play. When she was at boarding school, her father was working as a successful lecturer and surgeon at Charing Cross Hospital in London (https://livesonline.rcseng.ac.uk), as shown by the 1891 Census.

The strong mutable mode in her natal chart shows that she will have coped well with adjustment and change. The close contact between the Sun and Uranus would have stimulated an energy which would have made her determined to be distinctive and original in her life. As noted earlier, the Sun conjunct Uranus aspect indicates thriving on freedom and liberty. Therefore, it is perhaps unsurprising to know that as an adult Harris was interested in women's emancipation and in her early thirties participated in the first suffrage march in London. This was the N.U.W.S.S. (National Union of Women's Suffrage Societies) *'Mud March'* in February of 1907. She also took part in another march of the N.U.W.S.S. in June, 1908 (albeit for a short while). Kate Parry Frye, actress, diarist and suffragist recalled that when Harris carried a banner which was "fearfully heavy … it was a beauty nauge cloth (a soft and textured fabric hand woven on historic looms), brown and yellow silk and cloth of gold" (https://womanandhersphere.com/tag/suffrage-procession/). She continued: "… Mrs Percy Harris was just behind. She had to fall out early as she went very strange and there were lots of people" (ibid) (dates for Harris marching with Union from Elizabeth Crawford at https://womanandhersphere.com – information to Author).

Progress continued for the union, as in November of 1908 Harris was reported as being in attendance at their A.G.M. Frieda Harris had married Percy Harris Liberal M.P. (it was later he became Sir Percy Harris). In 1901, he also was a supporter of the Women's Movement (Crawford, 2013, p50), thus showing his liberal attitude towards women and equality, as well as their rights. Interestingly, in 1911, Harris' mother, Mrs Bloxam, was on the first Provisional Committee for the Bourne End and District Women's Suffrage Society. Harris' parents moved to Buckinghamshire after her father retired from the medical profession.

Kate Parry Frye recorded that on Tuesday October 3rd, 1911, Mrs Bloxam attended and was sworn in as one of the committee members (Crawford, 2013, p72). Two months later, on Saturday, December 9th,1911, Bloxam met with Parry Frye in the morning, "She is full of fears about the Bourne End meeting – hears of gentleman supplying themselves with 'sacks of rats' etc." (ibid, p83). Clearly the women's group was gaining momentum and agitating the men in the village.

The union continued their campaign for all women to have the right to vote in the United Kingdom, having initially started their campaign as far back as the late 1800's. The nature of Uranus is ground-breaking, liberating and progressive by nature. At this time, Harris was part of a generation of women who determinedly campaigned for a better way of life for women. We know that her Moon sign is Libra, which is also associated with fairness, equality and justice, which indicates that instinctively Harris would have been sensitive to such themes.

Other symbolism of the Sun conjunct Uranus also suggests that Harris greatly valued self-expression and living her life creatively. She enjoyed an audience of a kind and any artistic endeavours that she undertook, she would have been proud to have done to the best of her capability, such is the nature of many Leos. The Uranus in Leo position shows she was highly distinctive and unique. So much so, that she may have been regarded as eccentric, unconventional and perhaps even peculiar by those outside of her circles. One example of her liberating self and individualism (and as noted earlier) was when her husband became Sir Percy Harris, 1st Baronet in 1932, this position made her *'Lady Harris'*. She rejected using this title and instead styled herself as Lady *Frieda* Harris which showed she was not a shadow of her husband and was an individual in her own right (as previously noted). Although, possibly she would have enjoyed the recognition of being a *Lady*, as nobility is an association of her Sun sign Leo. There are other aspects in Harris' natal chart which also indicate her need for freedom, independence and opportunities; these are Sun trine Jupiter and Jupiter trine Uranus. These aspects emphasise the message of her need for adventures and opportunities, as well as space, both mental and physical space. Also pivotal in her life was seeking spiritual truths and the aspect of Jupiter trine Uranus suggests that she sought and found meaning in life through unorthodox channels. This was certainly borne out by Crowley teaching her subjects such as astrology and mysticism, as well as the philosophy of Thelema.

In the mid-1930's, Harris had coloured her hair bright red, which back then must have been quite shocking and unconventional (http://www.parareligion.ch/). A member of the Cotswolds Chipping Campden community recalled Harris as regularly using the family dairy and Frieda was described as "eccentric and flamboyantly dressed with her hair, which was red, always wrapped up in a bright scarf" (Kaczynski, 2017, p11). Frieda's grandson observed that "though she may have been eccentric, she was not a fool" (Ashford Harris, 2018, p197). He also recalled that when he was a child – a memory that he had of her from then – was that she was "a gnarled old lady dressed in volumes of some flimsy material, which I presume must have been silk" (Ashford Harris, 2018, p11). This shows the distinct impression that she left on people including her own family. Her friend, the sculptor Edward Bainbridge, said of her that "she had a most amusing sense of humour and a love of the bizarre" (Kaczynski, 2010, p497). These examples show how bizarre and entertaining she seemed to some people.

FRIEDA, LADY HARRIS (1877–1962)

She may have caused offence to some religious followers when she decided to use the pseudonym 'Jesus Chutney' for some of her artwork, which shows an anarchic and rebellious side to her nature. These characteristics are also in keeping with the unconventional nature of Uranus. In 1929, the New English Art Club exhibited a painting of hers in London which was titled 'Tony Galloway' and it was signed by Jesus Chutney. Many artists have pseudonyms but Harris may have wanted to remain anonymous so as not to be connected with her well-known husband.

In using an alias, she hoped to achieve distinction and merits in her own right as an artist. This shows her independent and creative nature. She also used the pseudonym for other areas, such as correspondence, poetry and apparently the telephone listing for her art studio in Richmond (www.Brill.com/Aries/Whitehouse 2021, p141). This shows not only an alter ego that she created for herself but also how privacy was important to her. It has been suggested that her involvement in Surrealism possibly influenced her using the name 'Jesus Chutney' (ibid).

In 1942, Harris' work was hung in an exhibition called "Imaginative Art since the War" alongside prolific surrealist artists such as Ithell Colquhoun and Henry Moore. This was at the Berkeley Galleries in London (https://hermetic.com). By this time, 'Jesus Chutney' had disappeared and Mrs Harris, the artist, was clearly less concerned about her husband's political life and reputation, for she openly revealed herself as "Frieda, Lady Harris, wife of Sir Percy Harris M.P." (www.Brill.com/Aries/Whitehouse 2021, p141).

Had her mother, Jessica, still been alive (she died in 1926) and known about the 'Jesus Chutney' pseudonym, she may have been outraged as apparently she was very religious (Ashford Harris, 2018, p189). However, her father was a convinced atheist and would shout people down with *"God damn rot bloody nonsense"* (ibid) at their religious arguments. Harris' Jewish father-in-law also died in 1926, perhaps he may also have been offended by the use of the pseudonym, because of his strong religious beliefs, but this is conjecture. Even if offense had been caused to family members, it seems unlikely that would have changed her mind about calling herself 'Jesus Chutney', given her wilful nature.

Another example of Harris' creative and unusual nature can be seen when, in 1911, she and her husband moved into 'The Little House', Winchelsea in East Sussex and they became well-known to the local community. She had been described by the locals as "unconventional and unpredictable" and she was known for "getting up in the night and drawing immensely curvaceous nudes, in charcoal, on the white walls of the drawing room," as well as waltzing round the town in long nightgowns (Marlow Museum/Winchelsea Court Museum). Perhaps she worked best at night without any interruptions and she may have suffered with insomnia or she just did not need a lot of sleep.

Harris was inspired by the location – she illustrated and wrote a book called *Winchelsea, A Legend*, which was a short mythical fantasy and it was published in 1926 by Selwyn and Blount. The pictures are lithograms with four full-page colour illustrations which have a limited palette and use of pastel shades. Percy Harris equally loved Winchelsea and described how he and Frieda "would never tire of sitting on the ramparts, drinking in the sea air and the marvellous view" (Harris, 1947, p51).

ART, COLLABORATION AND DESIGN

Harris illustrated and painted the *Thoth Tarot* deck of cards for Aleister Crowley and in her creation she modernised the Tarot's symbolism and was unafraid to use contemporary art styles such as projective geometry to help achieve her final vision. However, when *The Book of Thoth* was published, Harris was said to have been angry that her paintings appeared as poor reproductions and that they had been reduced to illustrative status in *The Book of Thoth* (Churton, 2011, p406). John Symonds (Crowley's

FRIEDA, LADY HARRIS (1877–1962)

Frieda Harris (*right*) with Aleister Crowley and mutual friend, Catherine Falconer (*left*) c.1940.
Photo courtesy of the Warburg Institute, University of London and Ordo Templi Orientis.

literary executor) said of Crowley and Harris that "they were an extraordinary middle-aged couple ... she with her nose that reminded me of a parrot's beak, protruding blue eyes, and unconventional views" (Ashford Harris, 2018, p222). Note that Symonds chose not to give mention to the appearance of Crowley, showing how the female appearance was (and still is) a priority, rather than giving weight to her brilliant talents and personality.

In modernising the Tarot deck, it demonstrates her fearless and revolutionary nature. It also shows how her art, although not particularly appreciated at the time of creation, was recognised by future generations (especially those involved in the occult). This was progressive and is in keeping with the futuristic energy of Uranus.

Part of modernising the Tarot cards included changing (amongst others) the images which represent Strength and Justice. Interestingly, these two cards symbolise Leo and Libra which are the Sun signs of Harris (Leo) and Crowley (Libra). Traditionally, the Strength card was depicted by the image of a woman muzzling a lion (Leo), whilst the Justice card shows a crowned female figure holding a set of scales (Libra) in her left hand and in her right a sword pointing upwards.

Through the process of their collaboration, these particular cards had changed. 'Strength' was renamed 'Lust' and showed "a nude female riding on a composite beast." The rider is The Whore of Babylon, whom Crowley called Babalon (Decker and Dummett, 2013, p155). The Whore of Babylon is a symbolic figure and place of evil mentioned in the Book of Revelations in the Bible. The 'Justice' card was renamed 'Adjustment'. It depicts a standing masked, young and slim woman holding a sword pointing downwards and the scales of justice above her head in the cosmos and encircling the upper part of her body. The two cards also show the respective glyphs for the sign of Leo and Libra, as well as the symbols for the Hebrew letters Teth and Lamed which correspond to the two zodiac signs respectively.

The colours used in the Lust and Adjustment cards are amber, gold, mauve and pale blue in the former card; and jade green, olive green, sky blue, pale green and pale blue in the latter one. Harris tried to capture the essence of the numeral cards (excluding the Aces) "in aesthetic forms: they are abstractly light, heavy, happy, oppressive, etc. depending upon the use of shapes and colours" (Decker and Dummett, 2013, p154). The reverse of the *Thoth Tarot* cards show a Rose Cross (*see glossary*), the four points of the cross are: yellow, blue, green and red with rose petals in the centre point of the cross.

Crowley recognised Harris' commitment and skill in making his Tarot deck the best that it could be. This included getting Crowley to rethink some of his original ideas which can't have been easy but nonetheless she succeeded. As time went on, he wrote to Harris with affection and compliments, recognising her genius in the process of producing images for the cards and said "The result is

 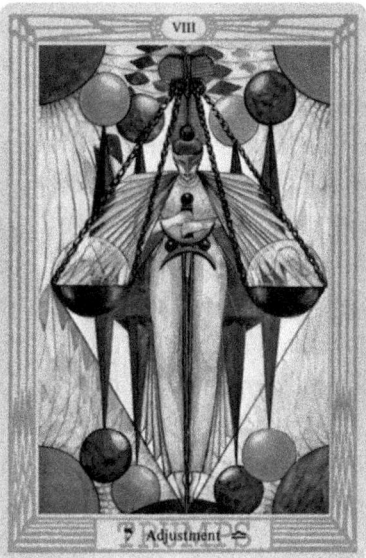

'Lust' card and 'Adjustment' card from the Thoth Tarot deck, with permissions from the Ordo Templi Orients and the Warburg Institute, SAS, University of London

that any given card is something immensely beyond anything that I have ever contemplated" (Kaczynski, 2010, p501).

Returning back to the astrology and to the aspects of the Sun in Harris' natal chart, the Sun is square Pluto and this suggests that she was captivating and also had an intense self-awareness. She did not approach life with superficiality. This is because the energy of Pluto is deep and probing. Her determination and forcefulness is exacerbated by the Sun and Pluto both being in the fixed signs of Leo and Taurus respectively, which are both indomitable and unwavering.

DETERMINATION, LOYALTY AND SELF-PRESERVATION

The Sun/Pluto contact indicates that she was a perceptive woman and subjects that gave depth and substance to existence would have appealed to her, for example the mysteries and the occult. She was clairvoyant and "sighted" too. Her son Jack revealed that "she was very psychic" (Ashford Harris, 2018, p1999) and she even prophesised correctly about the woman he would marry (ibid). Such insight is in keeping with the intuitive and perceptive nature of Pluto. Jack also had an experience of the afterlife (which is a theme also associated with Pluto) for his mother appeared to him after she died. After her funeral and on that same evening, Harris appeared vividly to him and thanked him for remembering her (Ashford Harris, 2018, p198).

Other correspondences of Pluto include betrayal and treachery. An example of this can be seen when Aleister Crowley felt that she had betrayed him. This was because in 1942 at the Berkeley Galleries (London) she held a secret exhibition of her paintings which had been created for Crowley's Tarot cards "with a new and unapproved catalogue" (www.Brill.com/Aries/Whitehouse p141). Not only was he deliberately uninvited by Harris but she also omitted "the source of her mystical knowledge" (ibid).

She did not want Crowley there as his already public disreputable name may have had a damaging impact on her social standing as well as her husband's political life. Clearly her loyalty to Percy's political life was unwavering.

Crowley felt deeply betrayed and hurt by Harris' actions "which sent him into a black rage" (Churton, 2011, p390). Furthermore, Harris, for her own catalogue, used the same editor (Robert Cecil) that Crowley had used for his own catalogue (for the Tarot paintings). She had him re-edit the publication without a mention of Aleister Crowley's name. This incensed Crowley when he found out and he proclaimed "Frieda's sneaking treachery bites deeper daily" (Churton, 2011, p397). Whether he felt equally betrayed by Cecil is unclear. At one point, Crowley had considered taking legal action against Harris (www.Brill.com/Aries/Whitehouse pp141,142), although that thought never materialised.

FRIEDA, LADY HARRIS (1877-1962)

Harris' tactics showed that although she was kind and generous (especially with her time for Crowley), at times she could be shrewd. The aspect of the Sun square Pluto is shown by this example of Harris' motivation. It shows the crafty, determined and shrewd side of her nature when her own position was at risk. She took control of the aforementioned situation which potentially could have harmed her and Percy's status in society. It also demonstrates the Plutonic characteristics of empowerment and secrecy and the unforeseen 'sting in the tail.' The aspect between Sun and Pluto shows that not only was she determined and shrewd but she was also not to be underestimated.

Eventually, after a face-to-face meeting, Crowley and Harris resolved their bitter conflict and were able to carry on their 'Great Work' together. Unlike many of Crowley's friendships, their relationship continued and she remained steadfast to Crowley right up until the end of his life.

During her visits to see Crowley at his rest home at Netherwood in Hastings (in the summer of 1947), she found him to be not only ill and weak but also "dirty and neglected" (Kaczynski, 2010, p548). She tried to coax him into paying for a fully qualified nurse to care for him but he claimed that he could not afford to do so. Such was her care and loyalty to her friend, that in September of 1947 she hired a nurse herself to care for him, sadly after employing the nurse Crowley died in the December. It must have meant a lot to Harris knowing that she had done what she could for her friend, going well beyond the call of duty as he was close to death. Harris was Crowley's unsung hero when many others had deserted him; she remained a constant and true friend.

She, along with another loyal friend, Louis Wilkinson, played an integral role as executors for his will. Harris visited Crowley several times (as previously noted) before he died; and during the final times with him even produced sketches of Crowley, one included literally when he was on his death bed (Churton, 2011, plate 54 opposite p227). After her collaborator, teacher and friend died, Harris arranged his funeral in Brighton and the service included a reading of one of his poems, *Ode to Pan* (Decker and Dummett, 2013, p166). She produced a booklet commemorating Crowley's funeral entitled, *The Last Ritual*. She ensured that her name was displayed on the booklet and given as the owner to the original cover (Kaczynski, 2010, p554) and she asked for "a contribution of $1 (approximately one English pound) per copy to defray printing costs" (ibid). A year on after Crowley's death, she undertook a wish of his by holding a curry party as a tribute to him (ibid), curry being one of Crowley's favourite meals.

It has been said of Harris that "she was probably the strongest, longest lasting and most platonic relationship in his life" (https://paulhughesbarlow.com). This is an indication of the enduring qualities that she brought to their friendship. Astrologically, it is an example of how the aspect Venus opposing Saturn can manifest itself through duty, reliability and trust, even through challenging and testing times.

HER INFLUENTIAL AND POWERFUL FATHER

There is another pertinent example of how the Sun square Pluto manifested itself in Frieda, Lady Harris' life. Traditionally, the Sun and the Moon were held to symbolise the Father and Mother respectively in astrology; but with the modern changes in parenting roles in Western society over the current and last century, many astrologers have modified their views on these simplistic associations. Having said that, however, the Sun square Pluto aspect in Harris' chart is extremely accurate in describing her father.

It has been observed that the square aspect between the Sun and Pluto in a natal chart can indicate the nature of the father's work and it would have embodied the principles of Pluto (Tompkins, 1989, p123). This is borne out in Harris' case as her father, John Astley Bloxam, held positions of power; as well as his work being exposed to some of the taboos of society (ibid), which are areas associated with Pluto.

Harris' father was a qualified general surgeon and held specific surgical qualifications of MRCS (Member of the Royal College of Surgeons), FRCS (Fellowship of the Royal College of Surgeons) and LSA (License of the Society of Apothecaries). He made a distinctive mark in his medical career when he decided to specialise in the treatment of venereal diseases rather than general surgery. He surpassed himself in the area of "plastic surgery necessary to repair the noses and lips of those who had been the subjects of syphilitic ulceration" (https://livesonline.rcseng.ac.uk).

He was educated at St. Bartholomew's hospital in London where he became House Surgeon and Private Assistant to Sir James Paget (who became known for naming Paget's disease) and afterwards he worked as a chloroformist at the same hospital. In the mid-1860's he worked in the Army and also the Royal Horse Guards Blue as an Assistant Surgeon (ibid).

Other positions of power in his life included being Commissioner of the Peace in his hometown of Buckinghamshire in 1908. Another example can be seen whereby in the same year, having donated money to the organisation The Order of St. John (an organisation that rewards humanitarian work), he became an Honorary Associate. Then in 1912 he was invested as a Knight of Grace in the organisation because of his contributions to the field of medicine. In becoming a Knight of Grace he had jumped two lower ranks in the process (The Museum of the Order of St. John). This shows the Order considered his medicinal work of tremendous influence to humanity and that he had influential and potent abilities, particularly in the area of health.

After his retirement, he became interested in community matters and was elected Chairman of Little Marlow Parish Council (ibid). All of the aforementioned positions and titles show that he was still driven to make a difference in society and that potentially he could use his status to make an effect, which is also in keeping with the empowering, healing and transforming nature of Pluto. These areas of Mr. Bloxam's career provide evidence to support the observation made that the Sun square Pluto aspect can indicate the nature of one's father's work in a natal chart and embrace the areas associated with Pluto; this was certainly the case for Frieda, Lady Harris.

HEALTH AND ILL-HEALTH

It is possible that she also had an interest in health, like her father. This is broadly shown in her natal chart with Mercury positioned in Virgo, the sign which is associated with health and hygiene as well as work. Like most people, Harris was not without health challenges. For example, when she was in her late sixties, she had injured her back and was given a doctor's certificate to say that she was injured and must not walk or carry heavy things (Whitehouse, 2018, p17). Whilst staying with her friend Ram Gopal in India, he introduced her to a masseuse who was able to assist with some of her health problems. Harris said, "I was English and it seemed a strange idea to let this dark strange man massage me" (Ashford Harris, 1985, p262). Nonetheless, they went ahead and she described how "he pummelled my neck, my back, my knees and worked the muscles scientifically, all the time covering me with a blanket as if he were a Sunday school teacher" (ibid). This shows a certain modesty and shyness on her part, but also a professional standard employed by the masseuse. The experience was obviously beneficial, as after that first experience she said, "I was refreshed beyond measure" (ibid). She then decided to have daily treatment with the masseuse.

Her optimistic and pragmatic nature helped her to overcome any initial discernment about the masseuse and her reluctance about her body being touched by a stranger. Interestingly, in medical astrology the back is associated with the sign of Leo and many people of this Sun sign have experienced issues and weaknesses with their back. Harris made a good decision in having massage treatments, which would have helped her relax as well as tending to any physical ailments.

There is a quincunx aspect in her natal chart created between the Sun and Saturn – quincunxes often allude to health issues that can manifest in one's life. Astrologer, Robert Hand, observed that with this particular aspect people must learn to relax and that some could have poor circulation and digestion (Hand, 1974, p232). It seems that Harris did find it difficult to unwind as we can tell from her letters to Crowley regarding her role as mother and wife, whilst multitasking with the time-consuming task of painting the images for the *Thoth Tarot* deck.

Hand's observation was also correct also about some people having poor circulation. This manifested for Harris in her suffering with chilblains, a condition that can arise from a combination of cold weather and poor circulation. Elderly people are particularly susceptible to this. It must have been irritating and painful when she was standing to paint (if she indeed she did stand when she painted) and possibly made it difficult to concentrate. Harris gave reference to chilblains in a letter to Crowley.

He had asked her to paint a lady in the style that artist Aubrey Beardsley would have painted, in the hope that it may inspire her work for one of the Tarot cards that she was working on. Harris was incensed by Crowley's suggestion and on 29th December, 1939, replied and wrote to him: "Dear Aleister, *Know what you won't shall do shall be the whole of my Law!* I can bear many things, chilblains included, but I will not draw a lady like Aubrey Beardsley" (Churton, 2021, p138). Her rage did not stop there and she went on to say that he (Beardsley) produced "lifeless ladies which make me vomit" (ibid), clearly she knew what art and artists she liked and didn't like!

EXUBERANCE, OPTIMISM AND MYSTICISM

The Sun is trine Jupiter and the Moon (*if* she was born around noon) would have been sextile (*see glossary*) by sign to Jupiter. This indicates that Harris was naturally exuberant, flamboyant and found it easy to express herself. She was confident enough to deal with any stressful elements in her life (albeit with a strong, nervous energy and restlessness). As previously stated, Jupiter is in its ruling sign Sagittarius and this shows that Harris was philosophical, enjoyed adventures and freedom, exploration and travel.

This position also shows that she was optimistic, and had the ability to see life from a broad perspective, as well as being inspired by the higher principles which informed life. She had tremendous faith in life and pursued Eastern mysticism and religion. For example; Buddhism, Hinduism and the Qabalah. Apparently, when she was approximately ten years old she had a "dhyana experience in a gorse field" (Churton, 2021, p254). Dhyana is a Sanskrit word meaning 'meditation' (https://www.yogapedia.com).

Harris was also relatively adept at the divination practice of the I-Ching and had been introduced to the art by Aleister Crowley (although he referred to it as 'Yi-King'). Her interest in such areas may have led her to explore subjects such as Eastern astrology, as well as concepts such as karma, past-lives and reincarnation. Her interest in learning about these subjects when she was an adult is pertinent to the Jupiter principle of Higher Education.

Harris may (or may not) have known that in one's natal chart there are symbolic points called the Moon's nodes. The north node is known as the 'Dragon's Head', and the south node the 'Dragon's Tail'. They are believed to be karmic points which provide insight as to why an individual has been born at a particular time and what qualities one should be developing in order to advance spiritual progress in their current life.

In her own natal chart, Harris' north node is in Pisces and the south node in the sign of Virgo. These positions advise that she should try and develop her artistic and intuitive abilities as well as developing qualities of compassion and understanding, whilst trying not to worry excessively and discriminate against others. The south node (in this case Virgo) shows accumulated effects and residue of behaviour from a previous incarnation.

Astrologer and author, Victor Olliver observed that with the aforementioned polarity of the north node in Pisces and south node in Virgo "often priorities are warped by excessive preoccupation with detail and practicalities … what is needed is also a higher perspective, one that sees the bigger picture" (Olliver, 2022, p44). We can see through the content of some of her letters to Crowley that she was concerned with the minutiae involved in the process of painting the images of the *Thoth Tarot* deck, as well as the mundane activities of being a homemaker and wife to her politician husband.

Astrologer and author, Martin Schulman, observed that Pisces/Virgo nodes are the hardest position to deal with "as a result of many lifetimes, the individual starts to realize his own rigidity" (Schulman, 1977, p60). He continues that the subject is confronted with "the realization that truth extends beyond what his finite senses can measure" (ibid). In other words, truths such as faith and spirituality will overcome any analytical and judgemental attitudes that Harris may have had. In doing so, this would have helped her to progress in her (then) current life.

Chiron is an asteroid and is positioned (retrograde) in Taurus in her natal chart. It is also conjunct Neptune, as well as being trine the south node of Virgo. These positions suggest that she may have encountered situations where she had to be industrious and of service to others in a practical way. As she grew older, this may have become more prominent in her life. This is certainly borne out with her relationship with her husband, as well as her collaborator and friend, Aleister Crowley. Also, attitudes and behaviour showing analytical behaviour may have become foremost in her life as she approached adulthood, as these are characteristics associated with Virgo.

As previously discussed, Chiron is in Taurus which is an earthy and practical sign. The contact made with Chiron and the south node suggests possibly those previous incarnations and themes associated with it may have impacted on specific areas in her life. This may have manifested, for example, with areas such as caution with money and materialism, clinging on to people and possessions and also insecurities about her body. This is because those areas are associated with Taurus and its ruler, Venus. As Chiron is conjunct Neptune in her natal chart, it suggests that Harris may also have had a receptiveness and natural inclination to areas such as artistry, healing and spirituality, which we know to have been true and prominent in her life.

CULTURE, HIGHER EDUCATION AND POLITICS

Returning now to Jupiter in her natal chart and its trine aspect created with Uranus, it suggests that she had radical ideas and had a belief in freedom and liberty. It also shows that she may have found her meaning in life through more seemingly unusual or unorthodox channels. This is borne out, for example, with her involvement and support of the Suffragist movement (which was revolutionary at the time) and her memberships in mystical orders as well as being a Co-Mason.

She also found herself on the fringe of politics in being a politician's wife; she obligatorily supported her husband and his extensive involvement with the Liberal Party. As previously noted, he became Liberal Chief Whip and then Deputy Leader of the Liberal Parliamentary Party. His political life started in 1906 and he died in 1952, Frieda died ten years later. Later, when reflecting upon her earlier life, she wrote that she found mimicry of real life through the stage as well as the House of Commons, both of which addressed human affairs (Ashford Harris, 2018, p249), but in them she claimed that she found "no religion and very little gaiety and I wanted both then" (ibid).

During her life, Harris travelled to places such as India and New Zealand and also places nearer to England, such as France, Italy and Spain. She had a strong interest in Egypt and Egyptology, which no doubt furthered her passion for Crowley's Tarot cards, which were also called *The Egyptian Tarot*. Different cultures, religion and spirituality would have appealed to the explorative and questing side of her nature, which was part of the reason she emigrated to India in her perennial years. This is an example of her astrology in action, by way of the Sun trine Jupiter aspect in her natal chart.

Mars is square Jupiter in her natal chart and suggests that she could fight for her beliefs as well as attacking beliefs which she found incredible. It also shows that she had strong political and religious convictions. Although she had an interest in different cultures and religions, when it came to her own family, there seems to have been differences between her and Percy Harris upon the subject of educating their sons, particularly on a specific religious issue.

This can be seen from the following example: according to a family anecdote, one day a Rabbi called at the family home. Percy had sent him there to teach their young sons Hebrew. Harris refused to let him into their home and turned him away (information to Author from Ashford Harris, grandson of Frieda and Percy Harris). It seems there had been no discussion between Mr and Mrs Harris about the faith into which their sons were to be raised and clearly Frieda was annoyed with her husband's decision.

Percy and his family wanted the Jewish faith to be continued down the family line; it would seem that Frieda had other ideas and she did not convert to the faith. Certainly, her father-in-law wanted the faith to be continued down the family line, which is evident in his will (*see detail of will further on*). This example shows how Frieda Harris could have an assertive and defiant (associated with Mars) nature when it came to her beliefs (connected with Jupiter). Possibly, she found the patriarchal faith a conflict with her Suffragist politics as well as wanting her sons to choose a faith (if any) for themselves. This illustrates again how independent she was and how important freedom was to her, as was the right to make choices for oneself.

When she and Percy married, they had a Jewish ceremony at his father's home. Gentiles are not permitted to marry in synagogues but can marry their Jewish partner in an alternative venue, where the service is conducted by a rabbi. The marriage certificate for Frieda and Percy shows that they were married at 197 Queen's Gate, according to the Usages of the Jews by Certificate. The witnesses were Henry Riseley, Alfred L. Cohen, L.C. Sumley and the official was S. Singer Minister & Secretary of Synagogue (For Marriages) (marriage certificate: MXH 615256).

The aspect of Venus opposing Mars in her natal chart suggests that she was not averse to attracting arguments and conflicts in her life. This is because Venus is associated with allurement, whilst Mars is related to battles and wilfulness. The opposition created between Venus and Mars shows antagonism and resistance and there is also a sense of 'opposites' attracting with this opposition.

Her father-in-law was born into a Jewish family in 1834, and born Wolf Hersh Schaglied in Poland. When he left there he changed his name to Harris, which was an anglicised form of Hersch (Ashford Harris, 2018, p133). Harris' mother-in-law was Elizabeth Nathan whose Jewish family lived in the East End of London. Wolf Harris died in 1926 and in his will he stipulated the following:

> *"I desire and sincerely hope that my sons and daughter will bring up their children in the Jewish faith, and that my*

grandchildren will remain in the Jewish faith, and will marry persons holding that faith, and I should like my two sons to keep up my subscriptions to Jewish charities, including schools" (Evening Post, London, 02/08/1926, page number unknown). His estate was said to be valued at £263,393 which was an absolute fortune in those days.

One example of Frieda's religious persuasion was being a devotee to the unconventional Christian Science Movement. This was established by the American, Mary Baker Eddy, who had groundbreaking ideas about health and spirituality. Harris' eldest son, Jack, as a small boy suffered terribly with tonsillitis and adenoids and had difficulty breathing (Ashford Harris, 2018, p193).

Instead of turning to conventional medicine, Harris turned to a Christian Science practitioner who prayed over Jack in the hope that his condition would be remedied. It failed. Eventually, when Jack was sixteen, he had his tonsils and adenoids removed (ibid). After that, Jack apparently held resentment to what he called 'medical quackery' (ibid). Seemingly, his mother battled through with belief and conviction that the unorthodox practice would eventually heal her son.

As previously noted, law and politics, beliefs and religion are all areas associated with Jupiter/Sagittarius, whilst assertion and drive, passion and vigour are all qualities associated with fiery Mars. Harris was described by one of her anthroposophy teachers, Olive Whicher, as being "a woman of liberal politics, and had a very free-living, spirited and strong personality" (http://www.parareligion.ch/). This quote shows Harris' charisma, exuberance and freedom-loving character.

Anthroposophy was established by the artist, esoteric and philosopher, Rudolph Steiner, it is a spiritual philosophy and science. Steiner defined anthroposophy as "a path of knowledge, which intends to lead what is spiritual in the human being to what is spiritual in the Universe" (https://sydneyrudolfsteinercollege.

com). Studying anthroposophy must have provided a sound philosophical and spiritual base for Harris, before she embarked upon her innovative collaboration with Aleister Crowley.

OBSERVATION, PERFECTION AND TECHNIQUE

The astrological data also reveals that whilst Harris could see the broader picture of life and could be philosophical, she could also be analytical and discriminating with an eye for detail, as well as being organised and pragmatic, which is shown by the positions of Mercury and Venus in Virgo in her natal chart. Author and Crowley biographer, Richard Kaczynski, recognised Harris' perfecting skills and said that she was able to meet Crowley's high standards (Kaczynski, 2010, p501) during their working partnership of creating his Thoth Tarot deck.

Apparently, sometimes she would create several versions of a card before it was accepted by Crowley (ibid); the Aeon card is a good example of this. She wrote to Crowley: "I am insane with wiggling lines" (ibid), grumbling that she had "done about forty drawings" (ibid) of the Little Lady image in the Aeon card (ibid, p502). This shows her commitment and dedication in her collaboration with Crowley to the Tarot deck project, as well as her own need for meticulousness and an accepted standard of work that satisfied both her and Crowley.

She wrote to him stating that whilst working on the project, her "guardian angel shouts to do it the best you can" and "not second best in a hurry and you must hit a perfect structure to build the pictures on" (ibid, p501). This also shows her intuitive nature and that she trusted her inner voice when creating art. The aspect Mercury trine Neptune in her natal chart indicates her discerning and innate gravitas in the process of creating art.

Mercury is the natural ruler of Virgo (as well as Gemini) and its energy manifests in a way that can make one restless and find it difficult to relax. Mercury in Virgo also shows that Harris had a bright and sharp mind, as well as being talented with analytical, meticulous and ritualistic work. All these areas are associated with Virgo and its ruler, Mercury. Her friend (painter and sculptor), Edward Bainbridge, said of her that: "She had an alive and virile brain" (Kaczynski, 2010, p497), and from this comment we can see reference to her smart and quick Mercury in Virgo mind. As well as having an agile mind, the position of Mercury in Virgo also shows that she could be critical as well as having sardonic observation skills.

One small example of this can be seen when she wrote to Crowley about premises that she had retreated to in Minehead, in order to do some painting. She described the place and the other occupants to him as "a vast & hideous edifice inhabited by dim beige ladies in ¾ skirts & splay feet" (www.Brill.com/Aries/ Whitehouse p140). Clearly, she did not approve of either the place or the occupants!

One example of her other scrupulous work can be seen in her creation of three Freemason posters which were known as Tracing Boards. These works of art were produced when Harris was a Co-Mason. This organisation was a subsidiary of The Theosophical Society. As its title suggests, it permitted both men and women equally into the Co-Masonic Lodges.

Each of the posters represents the craft of Freemasonry; First, Second and Third Degree boards. The three boards symbolically represent moral, intellectual and spiritual development (http://tarotconference.co.uk). Harris blended the modern and the traditional in designing these boards which acted as teaching aids in Masonry. She implemented the projective geometry in the design of the boards whilst maintaining the traditional symbolism of the Freemasonry craft.

This form of geometry would have involved studying Higher Mathematics (aided through her study of anthroposophy) where configurations of lines and points had to be studied. During the process of painting the Tarot cards, she had to produce factors and images which included Hebrew letters, numbers, different scales of colour and illustrations and representations for each of the cards. Fortunately, letters between Crowley and Harris remain in existence, and one can see through their correspondence regarding the Tarot cards the level of detail that is discussed at great length during the process of their creation (www.hermetic.com).

This kind of detailed work and application of knowledge would have been satisfying and stimulating for Harris and is in keeping with the meticulous characteristic of Mercury in Virgo; it also paves the way for craft, specialism and technique. Harris has been described as "a skilled artist" (Crowley, 1985, xii). Some of the mediums that Harris used as an artist were charcoal, pastels and watercolours. The perfecting and scrupulous pulse of Mercury and Venus in Virgo would have given an energy, which would have helped Harris to produce the exact and precise result that she was working towards in her creative work. The spirited and visionary nature of her Sun Leo would have given her confidence and determination to help her achieve her aims.

Harris's commitment in the process of creating the *Thoth Tarot* deck for Crowley was immense and it has been said that "her success as his interpreter surpasses belief" (ibid). Apparently, she often painted "the same card as many as eight times until it measured up to his vanadium steel yardstick" (ibid). It has also been said about her that her long collaboration with Crowley led to his Tarot pack being "executed with uncommon brilliance by Frieda to Crowley's exacting design" (Churton, 2011, p370).

As we already know, Crowley was a Sun sign Libra and Harris a Moon sign Libra. It is unsurprising that they may have deliberated on areas such as colour, design and style for the cards, as these areas are associated with Libra. It is known that this sign can be indecisive and hesitant at times. It is also known that Librans like a sense of fair play and both Crowley and Harris would have been determined to have their say until they reached a just decision.

The Book of Thoth was written to assist in understanding the images and symbolism behind the *Thoth Tarot deck*. The limited editions were exquisitely "bound in Moroccan leather," "native-dyed from the Niger" and the "top pages were cut and gilt" (https://www.100thmonkeypress.com). No doubt the aesthetic and visual appearance of both the book and the Tarot deck would have been of immense importance and needed to be aesthetically satisfying to Crowley and Harris.

Perhaps their differences of opinion in part, contributed to the lengthy process of the collaboration between the two; as well as the need for perfection and of course the small matter of the Second World War. This sometimes got in the way of Crowley and Harris being able to meet regularly and safely to discuss the project. They did however, manage to partially overcome the latter point; by writing frequently to each other, although postal services were also affected by the war and so not as reliable as previously. Nonetheless, their sheer determination and passion for the task was unwavering and they continued as best as they could with the creation and development of the Tarot cards.

The venture had begun in 1938, the year before the war broke out and before Harris had settled in the Cotswolds. Prior to this, Crowley had been a regular visitor to Mr and Mrs Harris home in Chiswick, London. This was mainly to see Frieda but also to see if he could gain any information from Percy, regarding what the government's intentions were concerning the oncoming Second World War. However, her husband was concerned about his wife's well-being, for he wrote in his diary: "Found Frieda rather tired. I am inclined to think Crowley, who has been to see her, an exhausting influence" (Whitehouse, 2018, p16).

THEATRE PARTNERSHIPS

Her strive for perfection in her creative work is also seen not only in years of application and commitment to the *Thoth Tarot* deck, but also with the set-designs that she made for the modernist Ram Gapol's dance production. He was progressive and was one of the first to showcase classical Indian dance in the West, which started in the 1930's in London (although the production that Harris was involved with was performed in the mid-1950's). No doubt Harris would have enjoyed working with another man who was unique and visionary, just as Crowley was. This production outlined a large ballet incorporating the life of Shah Jahan and with a backdrop of the Taj Mahal (Ashford Harris, 2018, p250).

Royal Opera House: "Les Imaginaires" ballet programme, August 1934, showing scenery created by Blanch and Harris.

She made models of the set-design and wrote: "It took me years before we were all satisfied and I was tired out. My husband had died; I was alone and without responsibilities" (Ashford Harris, 2018, p251).

The time she undertook in creating the designs for Gopal's show not only reveals her perfecting nature but also how artistically she was willing to adapt for him, just as she had for Crowley's work. This would have made her a great collaborator to work with and, interestingly, alliances and partnerships are associated with her Moon sign Libra, the sign which particularly enjoys one-to-one projects.

Another example of her ability to work in a partnership can be seen where she worked with her great friend the bohemian, Lesley Blanch. She later became an author, historian, journalist and traveller. In August, 1934, they were responsible for the set-design of a two-act ballet at the Royal Opera House in Covent Garden, London: "Les Imaginaires" (Wearing, 2014, p377).

The piece was described as a "Euclidian drama" and the plot "a sad story about a Circle's love for an isosceles triangle." It followed a course by which "an evil Star and a tyrannical Blackboard, Chalk and Sponge do not allow to run smooth'" (Boston, 2010, p37).

Les Imaginaires was directed by David Lichine and premiered in Paris (Blanch, 2015, p11). His style of the ballet being described as "Euclidian" indicates that in her design for the production, Harris (along with Lesley Blanch) would have been creating a set-design which involved using mathematical geometry.

HIGHER EDUCATION

This is pertinent to Harris, since she was (as has already been discussed) studying projective geometry (through anthroposophy) in her mid-thirties. Therefore, she was able to blend her mathematical education into her creativity, which is demonstrated not only in her set-design for the ballet, but also her Masonic Tracing boards and of course in the paintings for the Tarot cards.

Little is known of Harris' early formal art training, although the Harris family believe it *possible* that she went to the Slade Art School in London. Unfortunately, registers for the mid to late 1890's are not in existence to clarify Harris' duration and achievements there. Interestingly, Harris' co-designer (Lesley Blanch of Les Imaginaires) in October of 1921 had enrolled for a Fine Art Diploma at the Slade. However, she left after only two terms of drawing classes, before she was eighteen (Boston, 2010, p20). As previously noted, Blanch and Harris were great friends

Reproduction of a "Painting of Miss Lesley Blanch by Frieda Harris", by permission of the Mary Evans Library.

and before the pair collaborated on the aforementioned ballet scenery together, Harris painted her friend – which appeared in *The Sketch* in 1933.

If Frieda Harris did attend the Slade Art School then it is probable that she previously attended Heatherley's School of Fine Art. This is because Heatherley's was the only art school in the country that allowed women to do life drawing in mixed classes. It was the first choice of art school for virtually every female art student and classes were booked by the term. It would have enabled the students to prepare a portfolio of work before the admissions interview at The Slade (Heatherley's, archivist information to Author).

Unfortunately, there are no registers before 1907 for Heatherley's School (which was based in Newman Street, London), and registers post this year show no name of Bloxam or Harris. So we don't really know evidentially if Harris went to The Slade or Heatherley's Art School. Interestingly, and much later, other members of the Harris family did attend The Slade Art School, and one member worked in the area of stage design for a while, following in Frieda's footsteps.

Designing sets for the medium of ballet is quite interesting astrologically. This is because in Harris' natal chart, the positions of Mars and Saturn are in Pisces, the sign which is which is ruled by Neptune. Dance is associated with Neptune and in medical astrology the feet are ruled by Neptune/Pisces. The positions of Mars and Saturn in Pisces will be discussed further on in more detail.

KINDLINESS, VALUING 'ME-TIME' AND MONEY

Venus in Virgo suggests that Harris valued consideration and helpfulness and that in partnerships she could be kind and thoughtful. As Venus is retrograde, it also suggests that she may have needed respite breaks in her partnerships and relationships. This is born out with her husband, for example, when they separated for a short while in the early 1940's. It is possible that, at times, she may have had a tendency towards criticism and disapproval in her relationships, since these characteristics are also associated with Virgo. This is borne out by the aspect in her natal chart of Mercury conjunct Venus. As Harris had an interest in reincarnation, she may have been interested in what the astrologer and homeopath, Mrs Alice D. Fowler, had to say about retrograde planets: "Retrograde planets indicate the negative character traits that are carried over from past lifetimes" (Yott, 1978, p3).

One small example of her condemnation can be seen whereby she complained (and often) in letters to Crowley about when Percy used to come and visit her in the Cotswolds, where she had escaped to concentrate on her painting. She was critical because it usually meant that a social gathering would ensue, with her having to entertain other people and cook for them, when she would rather have spent her time painting, which was the whole purpose of her being in the Cotswolds. Crowley wrote to their mutual friend, Louis Wilkinson, on 6th February, 1942, and he described Harris' family as being "family vampires draining her of every ounce of energy." He continued and scorned her many contacts as "her horde of Bloomsbury-minded parasites, satellites and sycophants constantly poisoning her mind" (Churton, 2021, p193). From these remarks it appears that Crowley was protective over Harris' precious time and whom she spent it with; especially when it was time that he felt could be better spent working on her paintings for his Tarot deck.

The symbol of Virgo is the Corn Maiden or Virgin. It is an independent sign and even when involved in relationships this sign prefers to remain whole unto themselves. Her husband wrote of how he appreciated her having her own interests and not emerging herself into his life alone. He said: "I have seen so many public men followed about by their spouses … to me it has always been a relief that I can find recreation in talking with her on subjects outside political life" (Harris, 1947, p192). Fortunately, he was interested in similar subjects as his wife, such as art, drama and music (ibid).

Venus is associated with not only relationships but also finances and security. The position of Venus in Virgo shows that Harris could be thrifty with finances, making them go a long way and also that she had respect for money. It also suggests that she had a strong work ethic and was not afraid of earning her own living.

One example of her kindliness and pragmatic nature can be seen when for a period of time Crowley was financially embarrassed. She suggested that she would pay him a stipend of two pounds a week, which was a fairly considerable amount then. In return, he would teach her magic; this was to help her gain a better understand of the magical principles that were fundamental to his Tarot deck. This was acceptable to Crowley and so the arrangement ensued (https://rwwgroupblog.com). Towards the end of her life, she wrote that she "had dabbled a bit in vague magic. I had designed a pack of Tarot cards and illustrated *The Chemical Marriage of Christian Rosencrantz* with academic symbols" (Ashford Harris, 2018, p249). This is a humble and modest understatement to say the least, especially given the time invested in the project and the impact that it had in esoteric and occult circles, then and in the future.

Harris has been described as Crowley's 'treasurer' (ibid, p222) and on many occasions she paid for him when they dined out. They both loved gourmet food and enjoyed the experience of dining at different restaurants. However, Crowley could be assuming and ungrateful, for in his annoyance he wrote in his diary about her caution with money. For example: "Frieda kicking about cost of supper" (ibid, p221) and: "FH's churlish hysteria ... it is only her insane reactions about money that do harm" (ibid, p219). Clearly he did not appreciate her sensible attitude towards money and being questioned about it by her. He wrote in his diary that she was "insane, bullying and threatening" (ibid, p219). His management of money, his and other people's, was clearly poles apart from Harris' responsible attitude towards finances and disposable income.

During the Second World War, when clothing, food, petrol and use of the telephone was all rationed; she had to reprimand Crowley and wrote to him: "I am rationed for petrol so I can't fetch and carry you." She continued: "I am limited to 3 minutes on the telephone price 2/– any time" (Whitehouse, 2018, p16).

Although Harris lived in relative luxury (with her family and servants, for example), she was also able to adapt to living a frugal life, when, for example, in 1939 she retreated to the Cotswolds countryside from London during the Second World War. This was to avoid the compulsory blackouts and threats of German air-raids and where she could devote herself to painting

(Kaczynski, 2017, p7). For a while she was forced to live in a caravan whilst essential works were being carried out in her adjacent country home, Rolling Stone Orchard. When she first moved into her home, she lived alone with no servant (which was a change) and there were no friends in the area. She lived in the top of the garage there, with no electric lighting (only gas), no drainage and no hot water and without telephone and wireless (ibid). She must have been desperate to get away from London and was prepared to sacrifice from her normal privileged city life, whatever the consequences.

This secluded and sparse existence suited her in that it meant she could paint without interruptions. She wrote to Crowley: "I have more leisure time and have less disturbance by telephone & the nervous vibrations of a political life" (ibid, p8).

EMIGRATION, CHALLENGING RELATIONSHIPS AND SPIRITUAL FULFILLMENT

In her mid-seventies, Harris followed Ram Gopal out to Ceylon and decided to emigrate in India, which was courageous at that age and although it was a huge cultural difference for her, she must have spiritually connected there. She bought a houseboat called 'Starlight' which was on a lake in Srinagar beneath the Himalayas in Kashmir (Ashford Harris, 2018, p197). She had a houseboy servant who looked after her until she died there in 1962. He was called Shaban and her son, Jack, who had visited her there, recalls how Shaban had "learned to cook the awful milk puddings she liked in addition to the fruit and vegetables, which were grown on the floating island on the lake" (Ashford Harris, 2018, p198). Clearly from this existence she was living a very frugal life and seemed she was satisfied spiritually, having found a way of life that was meaningful to her; sadly it was not until her perennial years that she found such inner contentment and peace.

Returning to the astrology again, Venus is opposite Saturn in her natal chart and suggests that she took art and relationships seriously and that love and discipline were important in her partnerships. However, Saturn is associated with fear and so she may have feared becoming a 'shadow' in close relationships, thus losing her freedom and independence. The aspect also suggests that she could endure relationships and any burdens that came with them. Perhaps she was also tested in her relationships, as Saturn creates barriers and defences. Also, in her closest partnerships there may have been times when she created such obstructions herself. For example, she and Percy separated for a while in the early 1940's (as discussed earlier) as their marriage had become strained. By summer of 1944, they had managed to resolve their differences and were on better terms, although when she returned to London she did not stay in the family home at Chiswick but instead had taken rooms in Marylebone, London (Whitehouse, 2018, p16).

Time is also a key principle of Saturn and, as it is opposing Venus, this suggests she may have imposed limits on her time spent with her husband, certainly when she retreated to the countryside to concentrate on her art and to escape being a supportive politician's wife. Her husband observed her commitment and diligence as an artist whilst painting the Tarot cards: "She takes her art seriously, in fact works at her painting seven days a week and generally twelve hours out of the twenty-four" (Harris, 1947, p192). He also wrote in his diary: "The fact that my wife was so busy with her painting, made it difficult for me to enjoy idleness" (ibid). Clearly, she had to divide her time between her passion of art and domestic obligations which must have been burdensome at times. From this example, we can see the aspect of Venus opposing Saturn at play. Percy Harris recognised that at crucial times in his political life, such as election times, his wife was especially helpful. He claimed his wife "has been splendid at election time, when she has generally worked herself to the bone. She believes in my political star and could not bear to see it dimmed" (ibid). This shows how much she loved her husband and cared about his career and wanted him to flourish in politics.

SACRIFICE, ESCAPE AND SERVICE

The position of Venus in Virgo and Saturn in Pisces shows that Frieda could be a kind and helpful partner as well as compassionate and self-sacrificing. Mars is also positioned in Pisces which shows that she enjoyed working behind-the-scenes. This is borne out not only in her supportive role to her husband through his political career, but also through her own talents as an artist, designer and illustrator. She would have needed to escape from mundane areas of life, perhaps temporarily being reclusive in order to let her imagination create its magic. This can be seen, for example, when she deliberately organised time away from domesticity in order to concentrate on her painting and to escape from the demands of her husband's political life (e.g. organising entertainment at home and cooking for his associates). This may have put a strain on their marriage and Frieda may have felt that she was sacrificing too many of her own needs.

Mars is conjunct Saturn in the natal chart and this aspect indicates that she had qualities of endurance and stamina. Because both planets are in Pisces (a sign belonging to the mutable mode), it indicates that Harris also had the capacity to make adjustments where necessary without too much difficulty. In 1939, she bought the aforementioned residence called 'Rolling Stone Orchard' in Chipping Campden in the Cotswolds. This was specifically meant for her to be able to relax without any interruptions so that she could paint. She wrote to Crowley: "my spiritual state has been sadly neglected, perhaps because I have been trying to paint and live Percy's life at the same time" (Whitehouse, 2017, p7); she continued: "Now these circumstances are giving me a chance ... I have had 3 day's rest, the first in 2 years" (ibid). This shows how she was supportive to her husband and sacrificed her own needs in order to support him.

When her younger son and his father visited her at Chipping Campden, she declared in a letter to Crowley that: "Nick has come home on leave – I have been delighted but am quite unable to cope with maternal life, cooking & households & Percy & politics, so have been bewildered" (ibid). Clearly from this example, it seems that her own private space was invaded, depriving her of the much-needed space that she craved for. Despite her and her husband's campaigning for equal rights and fairness for women, in their personal lives (and certainly in this particular situation) Frieda was expected to execute the 'traditional' roles of women in the home. Seemingly, her husband and son were not expected to carry out, or perhaps even willing to undertake the cooking and domestic chores.

When Lord and Lady Harris were living together in Chiswick, however, she at least had some respite from these duties as they had servants in that abode. This shows the duties and obligations (Saturn) she felt in her relationship (Venus) but she recognised that her own emotional and spiritual needs were integral too. By purchasing her own retreat, it reveals not only her creative and independent Leo nature but also that she could afford the time (Saturn) that she needed to pursue her art, and possibly felt duty bound towards Crowley.

Venus opposing Saturn also shows how hardworking, practical and trusting she could be – qualities that Crowley must have grown to recognise in her, as over several years she worked tirelessly on painting his designs for the Tarot cards. She was a perfectionist and would have wanted her paintings to be the best that they could be for herself as well as delivering the ultimate images for Crowley's designs.

Saturn in Pisces indicates that Harris could be compassionate and self-sacrificing and would do anything to help the people close to her. The position also shows that she took spirituality seriously and that she needed to create boundaries in order to work at her optimum best. Her Moon in Libra also shows that peace and harmony were integral to her well-being and that she needed balance and calm for a sense of equilibrium. Jupiter is square Saturn in her natal chart and suggests that in her life she may have swung between optimistic and pessimistic moods. This is because these areas are associated with the aforementioned planets respectively: Jupiter is expansive by nature, whilst Saturn restricts, and so are opposing polarities.

Mercury conjunct Venus shows that she had a love of Venusian themes such as beauty and love, design and style, colour and co-ordination and that she had skills in artistic and creative areas, which we know to be true. Although she became most famous in esoterical circles for painting Aleister Crowley's *Thoth Tarot* cards, which accompanied his *Book of Thoth*, she also applied her artistic talents in other areas too. For example, in 1946, she designed the dust jacket for Crowley's book, *Olla: an Anthology of Sixty Years of Song*.

As we already know, she was friends with the famous classical choreographer and dancer, Ram Gopal, and after the Second World War she actually created the set-design for his aforementioned dance company's London ballet tour of 'The Taj Mahal' which featured the life of the Fifth Mughal Emperor, Shah Jahan (Harris, 2018, pp197,250). The set for the production was based on a lotus theme that Gopal had suggested (Ashford Harris, 2018, p250). Each scene was blended with traditional Indian dancers and was dominated by a planet or a sign of the zodiac (Ashford Harris, 2018, p251).

The celebrated ballet dancer and cast-member of the aforementioned ballet, Kumundi Lakhia, reflected later in her life upon the Taj Mahal production; of the excitement of the Indian ballet being the production to open a new theatre in London (thought to be the Royal Festival Hall). She observed how productions and performances (as well as the audiences) of the West were more formal than those in the East. She also said when discussing the production: "There was one lady, Frieda Harris a big painter in London. She did the sets" (https://www.sahapedia.org).

LEARNING QUICKLY AND SPEAKING FRANKLY

Mercury is opposing Mars in Harris' natal chart and suggests that she could be assertive, direct and frank in her communications; such are the characteristics of Mars. Another example of her straightforwardness is that she believed that Aleister Crowley's teachings and explanations were not accessible and far too convoluted. She told him this and virtually forced him "to reproduce the whole of his Magical Mind pictorially on the skeleton of the ancient Qabalistic tradition" (Crowley, 1985, xii) for the Tarot deck which he was designing. He accepted and enthusiastically agreed to her instruction. This demonstrates that she could put her thoughts into action and preferred communication to be clear and concise.

Harris was by no means a pushover and could defend herself against Crowley if necessary. One example of this can be seen whereby she wrote to Crowley in 1939 and in her letter she wrote: "I have to write plainly to you because I enjoy our friendship and your instruction very much." She continued: "It is entirely spoilt by your attempts to use me as your bank and financial adviser. I have frequently told you that I have nothing but a weekly allowance & that out of that I have given you all I can spare" (Ashford Harris, 2018, p218). This shows her assertive nature and also that she did not appreciate her kindness and generosity being taken for granted. It also shows that she had a respect for money too and did not like it being squandered. The letter also shows just how much Crowley was financially embarrassed, given his frequent requests to her for money.

One example of her learning quickly (as suggested by Mercury opposing Mars) can be seen when she first began work on the paintings for Crowley's Tarot deck which illustrated his *The Book of Thoth*. The task started when she was in her sixties and although she had very scarce knowledge of the Tarot she "possessed in her own right the Essential Spirit of the Book" (Crowley/Therion, 1985: xii). What was anticipated as several months work eventually turned into an endeavour of several years, albeit a labour of love. It has been said that she had to interpret Crowley's meagre "rough sketches" and "mere descriptions" and that "with incredible rapidity she picked up the rhythm" (ibid). Not bad for somebody who had little knowledge of the Tarot!

Her candid communication style is also demonstrated where at the end of the aforementioned letter she warned Crowley not to expect to make a fortune from the sales of his Tarot cards. She wrote: "Your books are wonderful but you must not expect the reading or money-making world to buy them, as they don't want to think" (www.hermetic.com). This shows contempt for the money-making world, but also her plain speaking and pragmatic attitude towards Crowley's unrealistic expectations.

Mercury opposing Mars also indicates that she may have spoken sharply and swiftly and at times may even have been impatient and impulsive. This is because these qualities are associated with hasty and straight-talking Mars, whilst Mercury is connected with communication and the mind. The many surviving letters between her and Crowley illustrate this astrological aspect perfectly.

Here is another example of her communication, blunt and straight forward. Harris delivered a lecture on her Tarot card paintings at the Sesame Club in London (approx. 1942). When addressing her audience, she said to them towards the end of the lecture that "we should be standing here all day long and be bored, to give an adequate description of the Tarot cards" (http://www.tarokki.fi/tarotpuu/2011/03/18/). This shows that she was aware of the concentration span of her audience (perhaps even her own) and that she wanted to retain their interest and keep them engaged. All in all, the Mercury opposition to Mars aspect would have been helpful in aiding her to be a direct and efficient speaker and writer.

In 1942, when she was living in the Cotswolds, she was invited to exhibit her paintings of the Tarot cards as part of Chipping Campden's community *Battleship Week* (also known as 'Warship Week') which was held to try and raise much needed funds for the Second World War efforts. She wrote to Crowley and told him of the assortment of visitors to her exhibition, *In the Face of the Tarot*: "They look a bit ashamed and awed or else they want their silly fortunes told. I could cry sometimes" (Whitehouse, 2018, p17). She also informed him that some of the patrons were "very stuffy old ladies & very ancient men" and "little boys who ask intelligent questions & go solemnly round and stare" (ibid).

Venus is also opposite Mars in her natal chart and suggests that Harris may have had to fight (Mars) for her art (Venus). One example of this can be seen whereby she organised exhibitions and lectures of her paintings once they were finished, hoping that a funder would propose to finance the printing of the Tarot cards (Kaczynski, 2017, p11). Sir Percy Harris seemed proud of his wife's diligence and artwork and said when the critics found out that 'Frieda Harris' (her signature on some of her work) was his wife, "She is immediately written down as an amateur and accordingly disparaged" (Harris, 1947, p192). He wrote that she "had an immense output of pictures and painted attractive landscapes" (ibid). Another obvious example of Harris fighting for her art is through her determination to achieve what she wanted to, in painting Crowley's deck, where she had to argue her case for her paintings.

The aspect between Venus and Mars also suggests that she asserted herself in anything which was aesthetically pleasing and beautiful and where colour and design were necessary, such as the *Thoth Tarot* cards and Ram Gapol's theatre set, which has already been discussed. There is another example pertaining to her projective geometry. Her teachers George Adams and Olive Whicher, whom she met whilst attending courses at the Rudolph Steiner House in London (in the mid-thirties) were teaching the subject there. Eventually, the three became friends and Harris inspired them to use "very hard coloured pencils as well as very soft pastel colours for work with plant pictures" (http://www.parareligion.ch). They obviously took to her suggestions, for some of their work is still hung in the Rudolph Steiner House (ibid).

Whicher described Harris as a "friendly and special person" (ibid). Harris also told them that she incorporated some of what she had learnt in their courses into the Tarot cards that she was painting for Crowley. She was described as the 'artist executant' of the cards and "she devoted her genius to the Work" (Crowley, 1985, xii). These examples above show that she was inspired and motivated and could take the initiative where her art was concerned, which is in keeping with the Venus and Mars opposition.

THE END OF HER LIFETIME AND ASTROLOGICAL TRANSITS

Marguerite Frieda Harris died in India at the age of 85 on the 5th November, 1962, and clearly she lived a long time, which is in keeping with her paternal side of the family. She was a determined and unique individual; sometimes courageous and eccentric, and yet in other ways she could be quite customary. For example, her children (like other generations in her family and class) were sent to boarding and independent schools. Therefore, in the sense of motherhood, she was not tied to the home as her children were educated and living elsewhere. She was devoted to her husband and supported him throughout his lengthy political career. They had a long-standing relationship and they had known each other since they were children, both families living in the same area. They remained married until

Percy's death in 1952, although in the 1940's there had been a short separation.

John Symonds (Aleister Crowley's literary executor) claimed that Frieda Harris, upon answering his questioning about "how she had stuck with Percy for so long" then "replied briefly in an undertone that she had a lover" (Ashford Harris, 2018, p222). If this was true about her affair, perhaps Percy knew about it and did not object to it.

As seen from earlier observations, her passion from a young age was art and she enjoyed subjects around art such as philosophy and spirituality. In her lifetime, she never saw the Tarot deck on which she worked (so earnestly and passionately) published. One wonders what she would have made of its popularity today. Would she have given herself credit for her drive and motivation to get the task finished, especially in critical conditions, i.e. the Second World War.?

Harris was adaptable and versatile, enjoyed learning and could be of practical help and service to those she was very close to. Had she been alive today, she may have put an end to some of the many myths about her dear friend, Aleister Crowley. She may have hoped also that the Tarot deck was not used for 'fortune-telling' but instead to help the individual on their spiritual path through meditation and visualisation.

When Harris died, she was experiencing the following astrological transits (amongst others); transiting Neptune sextile natal Mercury and transiting Pluto conjunct natal Mercury. These are associated with communication, the mind and health, so we could expect the transiting planets to impact on any of these areas in her life. If we had known Harris' time of birth, we would be able to see the specific parts of her life that the transits were impacting upon her from the house system.

Transiting Neptune sextile natal Mercury indicates that towards the end of her life she may have become even more creative, especially in the areas of art, painting and writing.

However, as Neptune is also associated with bewilderment and confusion, it is possible that she experienced dreams and voices of delusion which may have led to forgetfulness and perhaps even anxiety about her own mind.

Such insecurity may have made her elusive and even vulnerable. Her son, Jack, recalled how in her later years "Frieda was getting more and more eccentric and we were much embarrassed by her behaviour on a short visit to England" (Ashford Harris, 2018, p198). He continued that "on one occasion, we lost her and I found her hanging onto a marine outside the American Embassy." She returned to India and died shortly afterwards (ibid).

Transiting Pluto conjunct natal Mercury suggests that her ideas and opinions may have changed drastically and that any communication with others would have taken on a greater significance and intensity, such is the nature of Pluto's energy. She may have reached a new understanding about life. Any ideas and subjects that she may have been investigating may have become compulsive to her, as other characteristics of Pluto include fixation and obsession.

Transformation and death are also associated with Pluto and so she may have been of mind that she would die in Srinagar, her spiritual home, perhaps even wanting to die there for spiritual reasons. Perhaps that is why she made a hasty retreat from England back to India (as discussed previously).

It seems that she was thought of very fondly by her community and neighbours in Srinagar. Her son, Jack, and his wife visited Harris' houseboat *Starlight* after her death and he described it as "large and dank" (Ashford Harris, 2018, p198). He said that "Frieda had become some sort of Saint and her portrait was in the sitting room surrounded by flowers." She was buried in the Church of England cemetery (ibid). Seemingly, she had not ever converted to her late husband's Jewish faith.

ACKNOWLEDGEMENTS, CREDITS & REFERENCES

I am very grateful to Paul Ashford Harris, grandson of Frieda Harris for his kindness, time and generosity of spirit in sharing knowledge about his family and granting permission to use the photograph of Frieda Harris as a young woman.

Heatherley's School of Fine Art/Archive Service – for information regarding its history, women in mixed classes for life drawing / preparing a portfolio for interview for admission to Slade School of Fine Art.

I am very grateful to Elizabeth Crawford at https://womanandhersphere.com for detail and information about Frieda Harris' membership of the N.U.W.S.S.

Mark Hetherington, artist and illustrator – for art detail on *Winchelsea, A Legend*.

The Marlow Museum, Buckinghamshire/the Secretary for anecdotes on Frieda Harris.

The Museum Assistant at the Museum of the Order of St. John's – for information about John Astley Bloxams' membership of the organisation.

New English Art Club Membership Department – for information about 'Jesus Chutney' exhibiting the work *Tony Galloway* in 1929.

Curator at Winchelsea Court Museum – for local anecdotes on Frieda Harris.

CERTIFICATES

Birth Certificate: Marguerite Frieda Bloxam – General Register, PR8 2JD, U.K./Birth Certificate No. BXCG 672416: 13th August, 1877.

Rodden Rating 'X' – time of birth unknown.

Marriage Certificate: Percy Alfred Harris & Marguerite Frieda Bloxam – General Register, PR8 2JD, U.K. Marriage Certificate No. MXH 615256 on 02/04/1901.

BOOKS

Bax, C. *Some I Knew Well* (1951). Published by Phoenix House Limited.

Blanch, L. *On the Wilder Shores of Love – A Bohemian Life* (2015). Published by Virago Press.

Booth, M. *A Magickal Life – A Biography of Aleister Crowley* (2000). Published by Coronet Books – Hodden & Stoughton.

Boston, A. *Lesley Blanch Inner Landscapes, Wilder Shores* (2010). Published by John Murray.

Churton, T. *Aleister Crowley – The Biography* (2011). Published by Watkins Publishing.

Churton, T. *Aleister Crowley in England – The Return of the Great Beast* (2021). Published by Inner Traditions.

Crawford, E. *Campaigning for the Vote: Kate Parry Frye's Suffrage Diary* (2013). Edited by Elizabeth Crawford. Published by Francis Boutle Publishers.

Crowley, A. (The Master Therion) *The Book of Thoth (Egyptian Tarot)* (1985) – Eleventh Printing. Published by Samuel Weiser, Inc.

Decker R. and Dummett M. *A History of the Occult Tarot* (2013). Published by Duckworth Overlook.

DuQuette, L.M. *Understanding Aleister Crowley's Thoth Tarot – New Edition* (2017). Published by Weiser Books.

Gopal, R. *Rhythm in the Heavens* (1957). Published by Martin Secker & Warburg Ltd.

Hand, R. *Planets in Aspect, Understanding Your Inner Dynamics* (1974). Published by Whitford Press.

Harris Ashford, P. *Odd Boy Out* (2018). Published by Ventura Press.

Harris, Sir Percy. *Forty Years in and out of Parliament* (1947). Published by Andrew Melrose Limited.

Kaczynski, R. *Perdurabo* (2010). Published by North Atlantic Books.

Olliver, V. *Chasing the Dragons – An Introduction to Draconic Astrology* (2022). Published by The Wessex Astrologer Ltd.

Schulman, M. *Karmic Astrology – The Moon's Nodes and Reincarnation – Volume 1* (1977). Published by The Aquarian Press.

Tompkins, S. *Aspects in Astrology: A Comprehensive Guide to Interpretation* (1989). Published by Element Books.

Wearing, P.J. *The London Stage 1930–1939* (2014). Published by Roman & Littlefield.

Yott, D.H. *Retrograde Planets and Reincarnation, Astrology and Reincarnation, Volume 1* (1978). Published by Samuel Weiser, Inc.

JOURNALS

'Signpost' The Journal of Chipping Campden History Society: 'Cartomancy in the Cotswolds' by Richard Kaczynski, Issue No. 6, spring, 2017.

'Signpost' The Journal of Chipping Campden History Society: 'Rolling Stone Orchard – the Artists' Wartime Retreat', part 1 by Deja Whitehouse, Re-Issue No.7, autumn, 2017.

'Signpost' The Journal of Chipping Campden History Society: 'Rolling Stone Orchard – the Artists' Wartime Retreat', part 2 by Deja Whitehouse, Issue No.8, spring, 2018.

NEWSPAPER ARTICLES

The Evening Post (London Newspaper), 02/08/1926, page number unknown, Editorial re: the death of Wolf Harris and his estate.

WEBSITES

http://www.artsmarket.co.uk/greta-valentine/greta-mary-sequeira-valentine.htm – Accessed on 28/01/2019.

https://brill.com/view/journals/arie/21/1/article-p125_6.xml – Accessed May, 2022. '"Mercury is in a Very Ape-Like Mood", Frieda Harris' Perception of Thelema' by Deja Whitehouse. Online publication date: 14th December, 2021.

https://hermetic.com/sabazius/frieda-lady-harris – Accessed on 10/03/2019.

https://hermetic.com/crowley/crowley-harris/ – Accessed on 19/03/2019. Letter dated May 10th, 1939.

https://www.imdb.com/title/tt0046951/fullcredits – Accessed on 26/03/2019. Ram Gopal listed as choreographer.

https://livesonline.rcseng.ac.uk/client/en_GB/lives/search/detailnonmodal/ – Accessed on 27/01/2019.

https://www.100thmonkeypress.com/biblio/acrowley/books/book_of_thoth_1944/book_of_thoth_1944.htm – Accessed on 21/03/2019.

http://www.parareligion.ch/dplanet/stephen/claas/olive_e.html – Accessed on 24/01/2019.

https://paulhughesbarlow.com/frieda-harris-artist-thoth-tarot/ – Accessed on 24/03/2018.

https://rwwgroupblog.com/2011/05/19/women-the-occult-lady-frieda-harris-artist-of-the-thoth-tarot/ – Accessed on 25/01/2019.

https://www.sahapedia.org/looking-the-pulse-of-kathak – Accessed on 10/03/2019.

http://www.tarokki.fi/tarotpuu/2011/03/18/lecture-on-the-tarot-by-frieda-lady-harris-sesame-club-1942/ – Accessed on 28/12/2018.

http://tarotconference.co.uk/lady-frieda-harris-rare-posters/ – Accessed on 26/01/2019.

https://www.twixtearthandsky.com/Astrology/EAS_Astrology_Merc_Retro.htm – Accessed on 24/04/2022. Twelve per cent of population with four retrograde planets in their natal chart.

https://womanandhersphere.com/tag/suffrage-procession/ – Accessed on 07/02/2019. About colour of march banner and Mrs Percy Harris having to fall out.

https://rwwgroupblog.com/2011/05/19/women-the-occult-lady-frieda-harris-artist-of-the-thoth-tarot/ – Accessed on 24/03/2018. Harris paying Crowley £2 stipend to be taught magic.

https://sydneyrudolfsteinercollege.com/resources/anthroposophy/ – Accessed on 05/06/2022. Definition of 'anthroposophy'.

https://visualmelt.com/Lady-Frieda-Harris – Accessed on 25/01/2019.

https://www.yogapedia.com/definition/5284/dhyana – Accessed on 04/06/2022. Definition of 'Dhyana'.

CHAPTER THREE

Betty May (1894–1980)

Dancer, Model and Singer, Clairvoyant and Witch

PART 1: SETTING THE SCENE

"Betty May" by Ashley Basil, Creative Commons CC by 2.0

Researching Betty May's life has been challenging and this was from having to unravel the truth from fiction, of which there was a considerable amount of creative narrative. This came not only from her inconclusive autobiography, *Tiger*

Woman, My Story, but also from marriage certificates, newspaper articles, inconsistent details on parish records and contemporary genealogy family trees. Not forgetting, of course, the oral accounts from Betty May herself and those that knew her during different periods of her lifetime.

All of these things have made investigations compelling and almost obsessive, as well as deeply frustrating. Nonetheless, it has in no way diminished the determination to become more familiar with the indomitable spirit who called herself 'Betty May' who rebelled against society and her family background. Readers will see that her biography is far more extensive than the Crowley and Harris chapters. It reflects the intense investigation and research needed to correct previous information about Betty May, as mentioned above. Hopefully this will prevent Betty May researchers of the future from entering into a whirlwind of confusion and inaccurate information, as indeed I did when starting upon the journey of investigating the life of the woman born Bessie Golding.

Through the interpretation of natal astrology, we are able to glean what some of her challenges and strengths were, as well as what motivated her. This piece of writing also provides information about her later life as well as correcting a lot of the declarations made in her autobiography. The claims may have arisen from poor memory and unknown facts by Betty May, as well as blatant fabrication, not only from her but also the ghostwriter of the book. This was probably done to sensationalise her book, generate further publicity for her and to increase the book sales.

Betty May was a dancer, model and singer who worked mostly in London's West End in the earlier part of the 1900's (approximately from 1912). She first found fame as muse and sitter for celebrated artists, such as Jacob Kramer, and was also sculpted by Jacob Epstein. In 1940, a buyer bought the sculpture of the bronze head made by Epstein of Betty May, for the sum of

34 pounds (Reitlinger, 1982, p622). As it is a prestigious item, it may be close to fetching approximately 12,000 pounds today (G. Mitchell in correspondence to Author). Kramer was a portrait painter and exhibited between 1914–1938 (Johnson & Greutzner, 1986, p295). Epstein was born in New York and became a British subject in 1907; he was a painter and sculptor (ibid, p167).

She was also a subject for celebrated photographers of the time but mainly for Angus Basil. He was published regularly in *Photograms of the Year* and his studio was at 100 Tottenham Court Road from 1910 until at least 1940. He was a pacifist and refused to fight in the First World War (http://www.imagekind.com/). A photograph of her by Basil is held at the prestigious National Portrait Gallery in Central London. Apart from Basil, she was also photographed by partners Vaughan & Freeman. Aside from being photographed, she was also drawn by her Bohemian friend and artist, Nina Hamnett, as well as other artists, such as B.N. Satterthwaite, Michael Sevier and art historian, Gerald Reitlinger.

As a performer, her repertoire of songs regularly included ballads and folk songs and she also had her own freestyle of dancing. Apparently, at a basement club called Wally's in Fitzroy Street, she would take off her skirt and wave it about in front of her as she sang *The Raggle-Taggle Gypsies* (Pentelow & Rowe, 2001, p231), you can't get much more freestyle than that I suppose! In *Tiger Woman* she said "Dancing is my natural mode of expression. When I dance, I am one" (Betty May, 2014, p70), showing how she had a natural ability for dance and was not at all inhibited and enjoyed performing for an audience. She

"Betty May" by Jacob Epstein.
Photo by Ashley Basil, CC by 2.0

was distinctive to look at, with her (then) unconventional bobbed-hair and she had natural beauty, and with an exceptionally short height it gave her an almost childlike appearance. We can see from the following vivid descriptions and impressions of Betty May that she was indeed captivating and unforgettable:

- Her long-time friend (and previous lover) the author, David Garnett, who was close to the Bloomsbury Set, described her in the following way: "She was a very small creature with some of the qualities of a passionate wilful child. Her face was like a tom-cat's: a broad, straight powerful lithe nose, a large mouth, with beautiful even white teeth, broad cheekbones, wild green eyes set wide apart" (Garnett, 1955, p43).
- Denise Hooker (Nina Hamnett's biographer) wrote that "her sweet childlike appearance hid a toughly independent nature. She was completely unreliable, her spontaneous high spirits easily turning into a savage ferocity" (Hooker, 1986, p45). Seemingly, she maintained her exceptional looks right through into her late seventies and Eleanore Atkins (her home-help in the 1970's) described her as "a striking looking woman with amazing eyes" (personal correspondence from Ian Black to Author).
- Sally Fiber is the author of *The Fitzroy*, that is the Fitzroy Tavern where Betty May was a main stay and where the author (Fiber) grew up until her late teens. Fiber echoes what Garnett says and even goes further, "She was tiny but her angelic appearance belied her violent nature. Those green eyes could blaze with savage ferocity and woe betide the victim of her wrath" (Fiber, 2014, p25). Fiber also wrote about poet, Powys Mathers, dedicating a poem to Betty May in which he describes her as being "like drunk confetti" (Fiber, 2014, pp16,17).
- Author, Arthur Calder-Marshall, describes her in her mid-thirties: "Her unpainted face achieving beauty by the

clear curve of the jaw, the arching nostrils, the high broad cheekbones and the sharp, catlike eyes" (Calder-Marshall, 1990, p104).

- Hilary Spurling, biographer of Anthony Powell (a partner at Duckworth's who initiated the publication of *Tiger Woman*), described her in the following way: "Betty was a tiny tough East Ender with the dramatic looks of a gypsy doll and a ferocious temper masked by an air of melting sweetness" (Spurling, 2017, p93).
- Author, Lucy Merello Peterson, in her book, *The Women Who Inspired London Art*, said of her that she "tried to elevate herself above a destitute London childhood" (Merello Peterson, 2018, p156) and that she "spent her life trying to climb the ladder into proper company. She was doomed from the start" (ibid, p111).

Betty May was a member of the London Bohemian set of the inter-wars years and was a central figure amongst the original Café Royal cliques in Regent Street, London, where for a short while she was a Bohemian celebrity. She has been described as a "proto-type Bohemian" because of her lavish beauty and ostentatious clothes (Nicholson, 2003, p306). At the time that she frequented the Cafe Royal, it was also used by celebrated artists such as the Nina Hamnett who was also a student of magic (Hamnett, 1984, p176) and artist, Augustus John, as well as the critic, Roger Fry, and the sculptor, Jacob Epstein (previously mentioned). Betty May said of her early days at the Café Royal that "No duck ever took to water, no man to drink as I did to the Café Royal ... the gaiety and the chatter appealed to something fundamental in my nature" (Betty May, 2014, p44). Artist and Bohemian, Nina Hamnett, as well as many other celebrants including, Rupert Brooke, Nancy Cunard, Dylan Thomas and Iris Tree also used to frequent The Fitzroy Tavern in Fitzrovia, London, and Betty May socialised with all of them.

In 1936, The Fitzroy Tavern was at the heart of a notorious murder case which involved dancer, Sylvia Gough, and Betty May. Book reviewer, Douglas Burton, was obsessively in love with Betty May who he'd met at the Fitzroy. Sadly for him, his feelings were not reciprocated by Betty May and she refused his offer to marry her.

Sylvia Gough had been living with a young writer, Douglas Michael Bose, who was fascinated by black magic and the occult. He ill-treated Sylvia and subjected her to physical abuse. One evening, Sylvia arrived at the tavern with a black eye, she confided in Burton who was also there that she could no longer live with Bose.

Then, Burton took her to his home to look after her for a few days. However, one evening they went to a mutual artist friend's studio (the friend is unnamed) for dinner. Unexpectedly, Bose arrived during the course of the evening; impulsively Burton jumped up and grabbed the item nearest to hand, which was a hammer, struck Bose with it and Bose died.

At the trial, Burton was found guilty but insane. Betty May went to the popular press and sold them a story about her association with Burton, never one to miss out on an opportunity of making money through the press (Hooker, *Daily Mirror* report of trial, 01/05/1936).

Returning now to Betty May's entertainment venues. She was also a regular in Bohemian clubs, such as The Crab Tree where she and former music hall entertainer, Lillian Shelley, were in demand to sing and dance to artist Carlo Norway's guitar (Hooker, 1986, p48). The Crab Tree's clientele was described by artist and author, C.R.W. Nevinson, as comprising of "artists, writers, poets, East End Jews, men-about-town, dancers, cocottes and all the rest of them" (Nevinson, 1938, p63). Hugh David described the Club in *The Fitzrovians* as follows: "The tables and chairs were of plain wood, there was a small stage, an endless supply of beer, bread and cheese and an admission charge of 1s" (David, 1989, p118).

Some of the other clubs she went to included The Harlequin and The Cabaret Club and its later incarnation, The Cave of The Golden Calf, and The Endell Street Club. She frequented pubs such as The Marquis of Granby, The Plough, The Yorkshire Grey and the Wheatsheaf in London. Her most regular pub where she was a fixture along with other artists and writers, and where she could be seen sat in her regular seat holding court was at the Fitzroy Tavern, as noted previously.

The pub community remained pivotal for her, not only for company and a social life but because by then she was dependant on alcohol. This she developed after kicking her various addictions which included absinthe, then cocaine and morphia (Seabrook, 1928, p28) which she had taken before, as well as during the First World War. Whilst many of the Café Royal's regulars flirted with drugs out of curiosity, for Betty May "it was more than a fashionable indulgence for Betty" (Hooker, 1986, p45).

In approximately 1919, she was still using cocaine and on one occasion asked David Garnett to go to Heppell's chemist in London and buy her some. On another occasion, she asked Duncan Grant (Garnett's lover at the time) to do the same for her. Shortly after this, narcotics were made illegal to buy (Garnett, 1955, p46). The Dangerous Drugs Act of 1920 made possession of cocaine and opium a criminal offence, and then later the 1928 Dangerous Drugs Act imposed restrictions on cannabis (https://navigator.health.org.uk/).

David Garnett.
Commons Wikimedia,
Public Domain.

When Betty May became a senior citizen, she was living in Kent and remained in that county until she died. It appears that pub-life was still her mainstay for socialising. Some of the pubs where she regularly drank in Rochester included: The Man of Kent, The Star and The Queen Charlotte (various personal correspondences to the Author). Betty May was still confident to go into a pub by herself and it wouldn't take long before she was socialising with people (personal correspondence to Author). Her favourite tipple at that time was still whisky (personal correspondence to Author), although, when she was much younger, champagne was the order of the day.

She also gained a controversial and notorious reputation amongst her peers for her savage fighting, as well as in some of the National Press, where she became known as Tiger Woman. Friends had described her as "a bad girl with a beautiful face and a good heart" (Kaczynski, 2010, p383). Their explanation as to why they understood her to be worthy of the nickname *Tiger Woman* was largely from the many fights and her aggressive behaviour, and not always when she was drunk either. Her regular 'party trick' was to get down on all fours, pretend to be a cat and lap her drink from a saucer on the floor (Pentelow & Rowe, 2001, p231).

Betty May boasted that she gained the name Tiger Woman after she went to Paris with a criminal whom she met in London. He was called the 'White Panther' who was apparently a member of the L'Apache gang in France. She claimed that when she went to the gang's hangout, she was set upon by a girl called Hortense, who saw Betty May as a rival to her. They fought viciously and amidst this Betty May bit White Panther so savagely that he muttered 'Tigre' and this allegedly was how she got the name Tiger Woman (https://en.wikipedia.org/wiki). As we shall find out later, that part of her autobiography was one of many areas in the book that was fictional.

In 1928, when she was in London, she told journalist W.B. Seabrook that "people will tell you the Apache is a myth; don't believe them. I hunted with that particular pack for months" (*Evansville Courier*, 1928, p37).

However, later, in 1934, she appeared as witness for the defence at The Royal Courts of Justice in the case for Crowley versus Hamnett. She admitted under oath that "the story of her joining a Parisian Apache gang was untrue" (Churton, 2021, p37).

In 1929, Duckworth & Co. Ltd. Press published her autobiography, *Tiger Woman, My Story*. It was published again in 1972 by Bath: Cecil Chivers and then again in paperback in 2014 by Duckworth Overlook with the strap line: *'The incredible life that inspired the new musical'*. This refers to the writer, performer and producer Celine Hispiche's musical, *Betty May, Tiger Woman Versus The Beast*, which was first performed in April 2013 in Central London.

Apparently, it was Betty May's friend David Garnett who gave her the idea of writing a book (Garnett, 1955, p224) and she did indeed write a manuscript. The autobiography was only written up until the year of 1929 so was not a conclusive autobiography. Gilbert Armitage wrote the book for her, and she earned £500 pounds from it (Rickword, 1989, p123). The first edition was sold at 10s 6d which was a standard price for a book with plates at that time. It seems that there was a short print run of the book which suggests the publishers did not have much faith in it.

Sadly, part of Duckworth's archives were burnt in 1929 and the remainder then blitzed in 1942 (https://archiveshub.jisc.ac.uk/). In its first year of publication, one reader described *Tiger Woman* as: "As good a novel of character as I have read for some time" (Truth, 1929, p41).

Much less known about Betty May was that, she had strong clairvoyant and psychic abilities which she references several times in Tiger Woman. This clearly was pivotal in her life and she makes references to her gifts as her 'psychic powers' in her book (Betty May, 1929, p127). This area will be discussed in detail with examples further on. But here is one illustration to start with. Jack Lindsay, a lover of hers (in approximately the early 1930's) recalls that one evening, he and Betty May were about to leave The Plough pub in Bloomsbury, London.

As they approached the door to exit, "she took up the hand of a whore who sat near the window and held it a moment. 'You're sick', she said with a friendly sternness, 'you'd better do something about it'" (Lindsay, 1962, p128). The whore stared back at Betty May and looked like she wanted to shout something rude and violent at her, but she stopped herself with a kind of superstitious fear and looked at Betty's calm eyes. "She stammered and hid her hands under the table" (ibid). Lindsay also said of Betty May that she had an "ironic insight into the false and pretentious and had much warmth towards the genuine of any kind" (Lindsay, 1962, pp135,136).

Not only did Betty May have a strong intuition; but she also had prophetic dreams, was an adept clairvoyant and tea-leaves reader and had a basic knowledge of astrology (personal correspondence from Jane Dalley to Author). Certainly, when she was in her seventies, Betty May was self-identifying as a 'white witch' (ibid). Her mediumistic skills, coupled with her palm and tea-leaves readings, produced effective results and examples of this will be discussed further on.

Betty May has been described as "five feet tall and of a witchy appearance – she was not a woman to cross" (www.guttedarcades.blogspot.com). Publisher and writer, Jack Lindsay, was courting Betty May in approximately 1928/1929 when she would have been aged about 34. He recalled in the third volume of his autobiography, *Fanfrolico and After*, how he realised that she was a witch (Lindsay, 1962, p131).

One night after sleeping with her in her room, he awoke suddenly and he told her what images had alerted him to wake

BETTY MAY (1894-1980)

up. He had a vivid dream about elephants surrounding him, all stood upright in a kind of hieratic pose. The vision in his dream disappeared and Lindsay was able to return to sleep (ibid). The following morning, Lindsay learnt from Betty May that "she had been drawing blood from me to use in a white spell for the help of friends in trouble" (ibid). If Betty May was telling the truth about what she did that night, she had a very peculiar understanding of what a white spell was!

In *Tiger Woman* she recalls a conversation she had with a lover, where they had been separated for a period of time and then were reunited. He said to her that deep down he knew she would return to him. Her reply to him was: "You had that conviction because I intended you should have it. I possess that power, you know, over those I desire to hold." The intent here suggests that she had used spell-craft to win her lover back (Betty May, 2014, p91).

An example of Betty May's magical abilities and knowledge can be demonstrated by the following example. She advised an acquaintance who had complained to her that since she had moved into a new home, there had been nothing but sadness in her life. Betty May advised her to "cut down the willow tree, cover the trunk in salt and walk around it three times. Then, that presence will leave you and the house" (personal correspondence from Benjamin Levy to Author). The woman followed Betty May's advice and life improved for her. This shows not only her knowledge of magic but also how she could (if she wanted to) share her knowledge to assist others with their dilemmas. Where she obtained this knowledge from is uncertain, possibly it was from magician, Aleister Crowley, or

Raoul Loveday.
Commons Wikimedia,
Public Domain.

maybe she had a natural comprehension of such things. Certainly, her natal chart has astrological data which indicates that she was a natural in the areas of magic and psychic capabilities.

In 1923, Betty May, along with the notorious author and magician, Aleister Crowley, made national newspaper headlines concerning her recently deceased third husband. He was Frederick Charles Loveday (also known as Raoul), a former Oxford history student, who had a natural flair for poetry and a great interest in the occult. In 1922, he graduated and gained a first class degree in history. He married her shortly afterwards in that same year, on the 3rd September (G.R.O. marriage certificate).

One story about one of Betty May's psychic visions pertains to a photograph that was taken on the day she married Loveday. She describes this in *Tiger Woman* and Jack Lindsay also describes it in the final volume of his autobiography. He wrote that a photo taken on that afternoon in St. John's Garden in Oxford showed an ectoplasmic figure lying above Loveday's head (Lindsay, 1962, p132). Betty May described it in more detail as being "a ghostly form of a slim young man lying just over my husband's head. It was as though the form was asleep or dead and the arms were raised slightly behind the head, while the head drooped gently to one side" (Betty May, 2014, p122). The eerie photograph generated a sense of anxiety in Betty May and she feared that it was some kind of omen. Sadly enough, it was, and her fears were confounded about it being a warning and this is discussed further on.

For a short while the couple lived in Oxford at 50 Walton Crescent. Although, shortly afterwards, Mr and Mrs Loveday moved back to London. Raoul went on to become a student of magic with Aleister Crowley, much to the despair of Betty May. Apparently, she had previously met Crowley at the Cafe Royal in 1914, "and was decidedly unimpressed with the magician" (www.elisarolle.com). Sadly, Loveday met an untimely death (on 16th February, 1923) whilst he was staying with his wife at Crowley's Abbey of Thelema, which was a house used as a temple in Cefalù, Sicily. He had been advised by Crowley to avoid drinking the stream water when he went out walking, but he ignored Crowley's warning. The doctor, who was called out to Loveday, diagnosed that he had acute enteritis – an intestinal illness (Kaczynski, 2010, p390). The doctor "ascribed cause of death as paralysis of the heart" (ibid, p391). Betty May observed that Raoul lay on his death-bed "in the exact pose of the wraith floating over his head in the marriage-day photo" (Lindsay, 1962, p134). The vision that she saw in the wedding photograph had indeed been a premonition, as she had suspected. It is unfortunate that the said wedding photograph has apparently never been seen by anyone else, apart from Betty May and presumably Raoul Loveday.

Whist staying at the Abbey, Loveday had also suffered with a liver infection and malaria (Kaczynski, 2010, p381). Raoul had always been a sickly person. For example; he contracted malaria at birth, whilst living in Rangoon with his family (ibid).

Betty May's friends Nina Hamnett and Jacob Epstein advised them not to go to Cefalù. Epstein warned that only one of them would return if they went to Cefalù (Betty May, 2014, p148). Hamnett had concerns for Raoul's life, telling him that if he went he would die. She continued that as she said goodbye to Betty May and Raoul she "felt a horrible feeling of gloom" (Hamnett, 1984, p176). It seems then that both Epstein and Hamnett, like Betty May, also had the gift of prophesy, as their concerns came to pass true. When Mrs Betty May Loveday returned to London from Cefalù, she was met by newspaper reporters keen for a 'story' about her husband's death at Crowley's Abbey. The news-hungry journalists got their wishes and, after getting her drunk, she obliged them with a story and was paid a sum of £80 by *The Sunday Express* for her account (Kaczynski, 2010, p392).

Her story was that a cat had been found wondering in the Abbey and that Crowley had instructed Loveday to kill the animal as part of a ritual and to cut its throat. Loveday agreed, although aparently he missed the cat's throat and instead had slit its neck instead. The cat escaped from Loveday and was caught by Crowley. Some of the cat's blood had been caught in a chalice and then he (Loveday) was expected to drink it, which Betty May claimed he did. Crowley then oversaw the magical rite and it was from drinking the cat's blood that Loveday died (ibid, p392), according to his wife, and that was her sensational story.

Several years later, Crowley's friend, Gerald Yorke, claimed the sacrifice had happened, but it was "unrelated to Loveday's cause of death" (ibid, p392). Betty May explained to Judge Swift that the cat had escaped from the bag that her husband had been holding it in, and the cat "dropped out of the circle, and that was very bad for magic" (Hooker, 1986, p205). This shows some of Betty May's practical knowledge about magic and also the importance of ritual working and sacred space, such as consecrated circles for protection purposes. In April of 1923, Mssolini ordered Crowley's deportation and then "persecuted, poor, addicted Crowley floundered in Tunis" (Churton, 2021, p339).

It was the publication, *John Bull*, which on March 24th, 1923, famously described Crowley as 'The Wickedest Man in the World' (Kaczynski, 2010, p394); further lurid headlines appeared about him in the magazine until May 19th, 1923. The article which appeared in *The Sunday Express* on 25th February, 1923, described Mrs Loveday/Betty May as "a cocaine-addicted pub singer" (ibid, p393). The sensational newspaper headlines even led to American newspapers several years later picking up the story about Frederick Charles Loveday's death at the Thelema Abbey (ibid, p394) and probably increased Crowley's already notorious reputation.

In April of 1934, aged 39, Betty May appeared in court at The Old Bailey and again made newspaper headlines. She was now known as 'Mrs Sedgwick', as in 1926 she had married author and journalist, Noel Mostyn Sedgwick. She appeared in court in

BETTY MAY (1894–1980)

connection with what was unofficially called by the press (and others) 'The Black Magic Libel Case'. This involved a libel case between Aleister Crowley, author and writer, Nina Hamnett, and her publishers, Constable & Co. Ltd. Crowley's complaint was that in her autobiography, *Laughing Torso*, Hamnett made allegations which claimed that Crowley practiced Black Magic at his Thelema Abbey, which he vehemently denied. It was a sensational case and attracted a lot of attention from the press. However, Crowley lost the case.

During the case, Betty May/Mrs Sedgwick was called to the dock as defence witness for her friend, Hamnett. Crowley was described as "a flabby ageing magician in a top hat that took the starring role as arch-villain, while Betty May, the witness for the defence, was effective in the part of a virtuous young wife innocently caught up in the sinister antics at Cefalù" (Hooker, 1986, p198).

It was under oath at The Old Bailey in London during questioning of the *Black Magic Libel Case* that Mrs Sedgwick admitted that her autobiography was part fictional. When asked about the authenticity of her autobiography, she declared that "certain incidents had been introduced into the book to make it more exciting" (*The Times*, 14th April, 1934).

Courtesy of the Liverpool Echo. April, 1934.

On the 21st June, 1934, Crowley was arrested on warrant and charged with receiving five letters which belonged to Betty May Sedgwick. The following day he appeared at The Old Bailey. He was bound over on the 25th June with 50 pounds cost to the prosecution. *The Times* newspaper published information which was discussed in court about the authenticity of her autobiography.

Betty May confessed that part of the book was written from a series of articles that she had supplied to the press. Mr Constantine Gallop, defending, said that most of the book was "utter fabrication" (*The Times*, 25th July, 1934) and he also suggested that the book was fraudulent. He put it to her that the book was issued to the public as her autobiography and with the intent that that the public should believe it was the story of her life (ibid) and she agreed with the latter point. During the case, she claimed that the factual parts in *Tiger Woman, My Story* were the parts that deal with Mr Crowley (https://www.angelfire.com/ga3/thelema/crowley/un1934b.htm).

Crowley's solicitors lodged notice of appeal for the *Black Magic Libel Case* and in November, 1934, the case for appeal was in court. After three days of consideration, three Lord Justice's decided that Lord Swift's earlier judgement about the case was sound and upheld Swift's decision. Crowley lost the appeal as it was decided that the passages referenced in Hamnett's book were not libellous (Kaczynski, 2010, p483).

By 1938, Betty May appears to have disappeared from the spotlight of the London Bohemian scene. However, the 1939 Register (taken on the eve of war) showed her living under the name of Betty May Bailey (as an artist's model) in Wirksworth (a market town in the Peak District), Derbyshire, albeit for a brief period of time. The Author's research shows that there are no marriage documents for her with the name 'Bailey'. The register showed that she was co-habiting with Hubert William Barfoot (whom she affectionately called Billy) who was also using the fake surname 'Bailey' and was recorded on the register as a retired art dealer.

However, the London Society of Art Dealers, which was founded in 1932, has no records of him being a member of their organisation, either under the name of Barfoot or Bailey (correspondence to Author from the London Society of Art Dealers). Perhaps the couple used this fake name, as Barfoot was not divorced and couples co-habiting without being married during this period was much frowned upon.

Hubert William Barfoot was already married to Agnes Hart and had been separated from her for approximately two years. Diary entries by Aleister Crowley reveal that, between 1937 and 1938, Crowley became involved with Agnes for the purposes of practicing his brand of sex magic. He nicknamed her 'Bobby' and so Agnes became 'Bobby Barfoot' to Crowley. On Friday 25th June, 1937, his diary entry said: "Betty May has enticed her husband" (www.100thmonkeypress.com), the husband here referring to Bobby's spouse, Hubert. A further diary entry by Crowley on Thursday 20th January, 1938, states: "Betty May: wanted by police. Very just" (ibid). Clearly he had knowledge of why Betty May was wanted by the police, hence his final comment.

The name *Borfoot* (note the difference in spelling) *Bailey* was given on the 1939 Register and the name appears to be in no other documentation or records. However, the authorities must have caught up with him, as the name was later corrected on the 1939 Census. There were no electoral records produced between 1940 and 1945 and sources were very limited during the Second World War. This makes it very difficult to identify where Betty May and Hubert William were living after 1939. Interestingly, Barfoot had fought in the First World War and served in the Royal Artillery as Second Lieutenant.

It is probable that Betty May first knew Barfoot from London. This is because the 1934 Electoral Roll lists Barfoot as living at 17 Regent Square, St. Pancras (just north of Fitzrovia) with several other people, but it did not include his wife, Agnes Hart. As we know, that area was essentially Betty May's hangout. The Fitzroy Tavern was a magnet for the locals as well as famous names and between the 1930's and 1950's it became "*the* social and intellectual centre of Fitzrovia" (Basu, 2019, p20). Betty May did not appear in the public eye again until (albeit briefly) the 1950's.

In 1955, a notice was placed in a London newspaper by Duckworth, the publishers of her autobiography, asking if Betty May (or indeed anyone that knew her) would come forward and contact them via letter. It is possible that authors Guy Deghy and Keith Waterhouse may have wanted to speak with Betty May at the same time as Garnett, but in relation to the book they had written at the time, called *Café Royal – Ninety Years of Bohemia*. It was also published in 1955 and Betty May featured in it. They described her in the book: "It is not difficult to see in the 60 year old Betty May of today the young girl who captured The Café Royal with her uninhibited and indomitable ways" (Deghy & Whitehouse, 1955, p122). Betty May was a regular feature at the Café Royal, notably between 1912 and 1914. "She lived through the Café Royal's gayest decade within living memory" (ibid).

Her ex-lover and loyal friend, David Garnett aka 'Bunny', had by 1955 become a very accomplished author indeed. He used the pseudonym Leda Burke for his debut fictional work, *Dope Darling: A Story of Cocaine*. He used a pen-name as he wanted to protect the famous Garnett family name from the scandalous novel and any publicity that it may attract. The book was published in 1919 and the heroine was based on Betty May (Nicholson, 2003, illustrations p6, bottom right-hand picture). Garnett estimated that the whole edition of *Dope Darling* was in the region of 15,000 copies and although it sold out, it was not reprinted (Garnett, 1955, p197).

Apparently, it was Betty May who gave Garnett the idea for the subject of the book and he described it to his father as a "seven penny shocker" (Knight, 2015, p142), which was probably similar to a *'shilling shocker'* which has been described as "usually printed on cheap paper and characterised with lurid writing" (https://scblog.lib.byu.edu/2017/08/04/the-victorian-shilling-shocker/).

Another example, of Garnett's fictional work worth noting was a novel (published in 1955) called *Aspects of Love*. This was used as the basis for a musical by Andrew Lloyd Webber in 1989 and it debuted in the West End of London. Another illustration of his successful work was *Lady into Fox*, which was written in 1922 after *Dope Darling*, and this time he used his given name as author of the book (unlike *Dope Darling*). Rambert dance company turned his novel *Lady into Fox* into a ballet. It was performed in 1939 at The Mercury Theatre in London (https://www.rambert.org.uk/performance-database/works/lady-into-fox-wrk103/).

In 1955, Garnett was about to release his second autobiography, *Flowers of the Forest*. However, he needed Betty May's approval, for he wanted to include and write about the period in her life when he first knew her and when she had a drug addiction. Garnett's publishers Chatto & Windus were nervous about being prosecuted and wanted to avoid any potential libellous areas in the book and strongly advised him to seek Betty May's permission about the content in the book which referred to her (Knight, 2015, p413).

Garnett set about tracing her by placing an advert in *The Times* seeking the whereabouts of Betty May. Given that it was 1955, it is also possible that he (as well as Deghy & Whitehouse) asked Duckworth's to place an advert asking if anybody knew where she was. Very soon afterwards, the *Daily Express* printed an article that said "BETTY MAY" had been "found" (https://en.wikipedia.org/wiki/Betty_May) and Garnett clearly had been successful in his search for her. They met up soon afterwards at a pub in Chatham, Kent, near her home at Osborne House, 26 Star Hill in Rochester, Kent (Knight, 2015, p414) where she lived. However, in May 1957, she wrote to Garnett from her new home address of 23 Henry Street in Rochester, Kent. She signed off her letter to him as "Betty May/Bailey". She was still using that assumed surname from 1939; whether Hubert William Barfoot was still using 'Bailey' is unknown. We can only speculate as to her reasons for using that assumed surname still.

After 1955, Betty May disappeared again from the media spotlight and later died in 1980, aged 85. This courageous, indomitable and unconventional woman before she was 30 had been married four times, divorced, widowed and co-habited with different men and had a vast number of love affairs. She committed adultery during two of her marriages as evidenced in her divorce papers (see details further on). It would have been considered utterly outrageous and scandalous for a woman to behave in this way by mainstream society at that time. One example of her adultery is shown whereby in 1916, her first husband, Miles Linzee Atkinson (whom she married in 1914), petitioned for divorce on the grounds of frequent adultery with Hyman Coutts (real name Harry Melford). She and Coutts lived together as man and wife (while she was still married to Atkinson) at different addresses including 27 Litchfield Street, 21 New Compton Street and 14 Lorne Road in Brixton, and this was whilst Atkinson was away fighting in the Great War (The High Court of Justice, Probate, Divorce and Admiralty Division).

> 86.—HARRY MELFORD, C.R.O. No. 9995-14, was sentenced as *Hyman Coots* at *Marlborough St. Pol. Ct. (L.)*, 17.1.16, to 6 mos.¹ impt. under the Defence of Realm Act—attempting to persuade a soldier to desert and forging military pass. Pre. con. of importuning male persons for immoral practices on C DIVN., MET. POL.

British Newspaper Archives. The Police Gazette January, 1916

Melford (Hyman Coutts) appeared at Marlborough Street Police Station court in January 1916 and was sentenced to six months imprisonment. This was for trying to persuade a soldier, Private Alfred W. Allen of the Canadian A.S.C. (whom he had met at the Café Royal) to desert the army and forge military passes. Coutts cajoled Allen to visit him at his home (which he was sharing with Betty May whilst she was still married to Atkinson).

BETTY MAY (1894-1980)

Allen told his superiors what had happened and that they all went to Coutts' home. There he provided them each with civilian clothes for £1 and two forged passes were sold for 2s 6d (unknown newspaper reported with the headline: 'Forged Military Passes'). Coutts' plea was that he was taking drugs at the time and did not know what he was doing, nonetheless he was still charged with fraud (newspaper article unknown). Interestingly, a poem was written about the occasion called *The War Crime of Hyman Coutts* (http://worldwaroneblogger.blogspot.com/2016/01) by Jamie Mann. Harry Melford also had a previous conviction under his alias of Coutts, for "importuning male persons for immoral practices" (*The Police Gazette*, January 28th, 1916).

As far as we know, Betty May did not have any children. However, she confided in Eleanore Atkins (her home-help) about all kinds of things that had happened in her life. For example, Betty May told her that she couldn't have children and revealed to Atkins the following. She had married a "well-to-do man" (personal correspondence from Ian Black to author). The person she was referring to was the son of a (then deceased) vicar, his name was Noel Mostyn Sedgwick, who at that time was a journalist. He went on to become a well-established author and also editor of *Country Life* and *Shooting Life* magazines.

George Dibbs King Waldron. University of Sydney

When she lived with Sedgwick, it seems Betty May had wanted children (judging from what Atkins could tell from the sorrowful tone of Betty May's voice in that conversation) but sadly it didn't happen for her. Apparently, her mother-in-law despised her for being married three times already and allegedly made her very miserable. Betty May showed Atkins a scar on her abdomen "like a scar from a termination" she said. Betty May said to Atkins: "They took my baby away from me. They almost killed me" (personal correspondence from Ian Black to Author). It is possible too that she had terminations in the earlier part of her life. Possibly they were 'back-street' abortions, as birth control and family planning did not become easily accessible to women in England until the late 1920's and early 30's.

Betty May wrote scathingly in her autobiography about her mother-in-law (the mother of Noel Mostyn Sedgwick), she disguised Mostyn's name in *Tiger Woman* by calling him 'Carol'. Perhaps she did this to retain his anonymity and avoid any legal problems. She also veiled the true identity of her other husbands. One example of this is her calling her second husband (George Dibbs King Waldron) 'Roy' in the book. She also referred to her first husband (Miles Linzee Atkinson) as 'Bunny' which, interestingly, was also the nick-name for her former lover and constant friend, David Garnett. It is unknown where Betty May was in the 1940's but in the mid-1950's she was in Kent and still living with Hubert William Barfoot, up until his death in 1963. She remained in Kent and died in hospital, aged 85.

PART 2: HUMBLE BEGINNINGS ... AND ENDINGS

Betty May was born Bessie Golding on 25th August, 1894, at 37 Lansdowne Road (since demolished), Canning Town, which was then in the county of West Ham, England. By the time her birth was registered on 5th October, 1894, the family were living at 45 Portland Road (now demolished) at Tidal Basin (General Register Office Birth Certificate), close to the East End of London. Another Golding family address was 40 Portree Street in Poplar, which was near the gasworks there. The family lived at several other addresses too. George and Ellen Golding had five children. Bessie

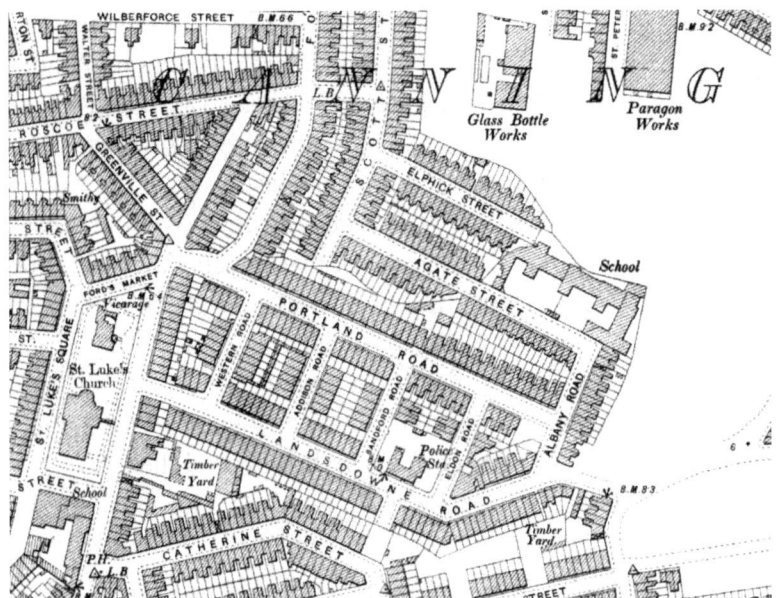

National Library of Scotland. CC by 4.0

was the second child, the eldest was George and then after Bessie there was Maria, Henry (aka Harry) and Ethel, respectively.

The 1901 Census shows that Bessie was not always in the care of her parents. At the age of six, Bessie was living on a barge in Northfleet in Kent with her great-aunt, Eliza Walker (originally from Limehouse). Her husband was Bessie's great-uncle, William Walker (born in Gravesend, Kent), who was a bargeman. How long exactly Bessie had been living with them before the 1901 census is unknown and, furthermore, why she was residing there is also unknown.

Bessie Golding received her education at Clarkson Street School in Canning Town (London Metropolitan Archives/ School Admission Records) and Oban Street School in Poplar, London and she would have been around fourteen when she left school. These documents therefore indicate that her story in her autobiography, *Tiger Woman, My Story*, about being sent to a school in a village in Somerset is untrue.

The 1911 Census of England & Wales shows us that she had left home (be that her parent's home or a relative's home) and it is possible that she had left whatever home she was in well before the Census date of March, 1911. At the age of seventeen she was working in service as a general domestic servant at Norley Farmhouse, Wonersh in Guildford, Surrey (www.ancestry.co.uk/1911 Census). She was one of five servants there and the only female servant. Her time in service was short-lived as in 1912 she was back in London and living at 10/12 Grove Street in Stepney. Interestingly, that Street is now called Golding Street. However, it has no connection to Bessie Golding or her family, Golding was a very common name in the East End then.

On 15th June, 1912, she was admitted from her home to the Raine Street Workhouse in Stepney. She was discharged from there on the same day but then admitted to the Infirmary which was a hospital building next door in Old Gravel Lane (parish of St. George in the East End). The discharge record from the Infirmary shows that she was in there until 13th September, 1912, so she was unwell for three months. Her Infirmary record simply states 'sickness' as the reason for her being in their care (London Metropolitan Archives). There is no detail given as to what her 'sickness' was exactly and it was certainly a general term that the Infirmary used then, irrespective of what the condition was.

Interestingly, in *The Confessions of Aleister Crowley* he wrote how he and Betty May spoke candidly with each other. He claimed that, "In her childhood, an accident had damaged her brain permanently so that its functions were discontinuous, and she had not mended matters much by taking to cocaine at the age of about twenty" (Symonds & Grant, 1979, p904). Whether her accident was the reason she was in the Infirmary when she was seventeen, we do not know. If this information about her having an accident is correct, it suggests that Betty May must have been on cordial terms with Crowley at times to share this private information to him.

BETTY MAY (1894–1980)

The various official censuses of England and Wales reveal that Bessie Golding's family home changed several times (as previously discussed). This was probably because of the appalling overcrowding, poor conditions of housing, lack of adequate sanitation and dreadful air pollution from the factories and chimneys. Charles Booth, social researcher of the working-classes in late-Victorian London and author of *Life and Labour of the People in London (1886)* identified through his research the following: both Portree Street and Grove Street were classified in his work as 'pink' regions. This meant that the properties in the streets and its inhabitants were a combination of being "comfortable and poor." Certainly, the aforementioned streets weren't the poorest; at least not when Booth's research was undertaken in 1886, although of course that may well have changed by the time Bessie Golding was born in 1894. However, had the situation not changed, it is possible that the Golding family were in the 'comfortable' classification of Booth's research, given that Betty May's parents and grandparents were in employment. The shortage of housing meant that it was not uncommon for families to be housed in single rooms where many of the buildings were falling into disrepair and often the properties had little or no sanitation. If it was a terraced house the Golding's were living in, there was often one family in each room of the property.

Betty May was *seemingly* frank in her autobiography about the poverty into which she was born and never forgot the harrowing experience of turmoil, squalor and impoverishment. Through much of her adult life she tried to avoid poverty, surviving at times from one day to the next. This was something her friend, David Garnett, observed about her throughout her life. He said of her: "She was spontaneous and changeable, pursuing pleasure wherever she found it and caring nothing for money as long as she had a few shillings in her purse" (Garnett, 1955, p46).

Reasons for the Golding family moving several times when Bessie was a young child are unknown. It may have been through being unable to afford the rent for their home as well as the poor housing conditions and sanitation (as previously noted) that forced them to move to more suitable dwellings. She described Tidal Basin in East London as "one of the poorest and most squalid districts in London" (Betty May, 2014, p13). She went on to describe in her autobiography how "the family lived in one room and how the children used to sleep on bundles of rags in the various corners of the room" (ibid).

However, there may have been more personal reasons for the frequent change of residence. For example, the Olga Street School Admissions in Bow show a George Golding (Bessie's brother) being admitted to Olga Street School, aged six. However, his 'parent' was recorded as being 'Barnardo's' and he remained there for three weeks. Farms used to apply to Barnardo's for labourers and it appears that George, the eldest of the Golding children, was then sent to Yorkshire to work on a farm at Low Woods in Sproxton, Helmsley, North Yorkshire (1911 Census).

He never returned to the family home, seemingly there was a crisis in the home. The children of the Golding family were further separated. The 1911 Census shows that Bessie's sisters, Ethel and Marie, were living in a boarding cottage in Thornburg, Gloucestershire. The keeper's name was Mary Smith and she lived there with her daughter (she was related to Sarah Ann Abbott's parents – Sarah being Bessie's paternal grandmother).

Clearly, Bessie had been separated from her siblings at an early age and they all had gone their different ways. It seems that all of the children never lived together, for various reasons. Certainly, the *apparent* disappearance and death of Ellen, Bessie's mother, seems to have played a pivotal role in the breakdown of the family.

Bessie was just six years old (1901 Census) when she was sent to stay with relatives in Northfleet in Kent and she lived with them on their barge. They also owned a house, so were not exactly poor. What *was* the reason for Bessie being sent there? Perhaps her mother was unable to care for Betty May if she was working long hours at the factory and having to run the home as well? The episode in Bessie Golding's life when she lived with her great-aunt and great-uncle in her formative years clearly left a significant memory with her. She recalls in vivid detail in *Tiger Woman, My Story* the time when she was living on the barge with her relations.

Apparently, they washed her a great deal, forbade her to use certain words, brushed her hair a lot and insisted she cleaned her teeth twice a day and taught her the Lord's Prayer (Betty May, 2014, p26). This infers that her parents never undertook those activities with her. Although she recognised a kindness towards her, she also felt ignored and neglected by her great-aunt and great-uncle and she was bored by the monotony of barge-life (ibid). One day she overheard her great-aunt say: "The poor child … has had no proper upbringing. She's a regular little savage." If that comment *was* made then it must have been bewildering and hurtful for a six year old child to hear. Previously to living with her great-aunt and great-uncle, she had also been sent to live with her father's parents who lived in Poplar. However, it seems there must have been some progress in Bessie Golding's family, at least for a while, or perhaps the relatives in Kent had decided that they no longer wanted to care for Bessie Golding.

The change in her situation is indicated by the following. In 1904 the Oban Street School Admissions Record shows that Bessie Golding was admitted to the school and that her father, George, was her parent. They both lived at 40 Portree Street (www.ancestry.co.uk/London Metropolitan Archives/Boards of Guardians Tower Hamlets is). Clearly, Bessie was no longer living in Kent. Interestingly, official records show that in 1903, Bessie's sister, Marie, was also living in Northfleet, Kent with her great-aunt and great-uncle. The sisters had at different parts of their childhood been sent to live in Kent. Ironically, it was to be the county where Bessie ended her adult life.

In a newspaper interview shortly before she was 35, Bessie told an American journalist, William B. Seabrook (who was in London when they met), the following: "My parents were nothing to brag about; they were shiftless and now and then they drank" (Seabrook, 1928, p39). We do not know if this was true or not about her parents. Then, in the same sentence she earnestly declared to Seabrook: "I was born Marlow Golding," which her birth certificate shows to be untrue. This is another fabrication and illustrates her shedding some of her past and giving herself a new persona for her own reasons, whatever they may have been. This was the same interview where she told W.B. Seabrook that he should believe her about her experiences with the Apache Gang. Seabrook was an occultist, traveller and writer. In 1940, his book, *Witchcraft – Its Power in the World Today*, was published. Interestingly, Bessie and Seabrook had a mutual contact in Aleister Crowley, who in 1919 stayed with Seabrook at his farm, which is discussed in the aforementioned book by Seabrook.

As we know, Bessie Golding started her life in Lansdowne Road and then Portland Road; both were close to the southern end of the Victoria Dock Road, which was near to Tidal Basin (maps.nls.uk/view/101019807). This area was at the heart of the industrious East London Docklands, where a hive of activity and a supportive community thrived. However, crime and prostitution were rife at the docks and the opium dens (which were mainly run by the Chinese) were rampant in Limehouse. It is interesting that Bessie called her autobiography: *Tiger Woman, My Story*. This is because the nearby Betts Street, near to the workhouse and the Infirmary where she once stayed (as discussed earlier), was long-known as *'Tiger Bay'*. The locals named the "feisty prostitutes there, *Tigresses*; they wore startling clothes and colourful boots" (stgitehistory.org.uk).

Biographer and novelist, Arthur Calder-Marshall, described in his biography (*The Magic of my Youth*) the appearance of Betty May who was out one evening with her entourage and hailing a cab, he approximated that she may have been 35 at the time:

"She was conspicuously dressed in a coat of tiger skin and a cap to match. With breeches, top-boots and a whip ... there was nothing unwomanly about her. Domination was not the denial of her sex but its prerogative" (Calder-Marshall, 1990, p104). He observed the distinctive dress style, including her choice of colours too, seeing that although her coat was not fastened, he could see that "a medley of bright colours was revealed so startling in contrast that it seemed impossible that they could harmonise" (ibid). Clearly, he was captivated by her flamboyant appearance, for he continued "and yet with a flair for colour like Romany, she had so arranged them that they were brilliantly effective" (ibid).

The subject of colourful clothes, fabrics and a shortage of clothes from poverty was an area she discussed in detail in her autobiography. She revealed that: "Colours to me are like children to a loving mother. Each is my favourite, yet I can never bring myself to deny the others by preferring one" (Betty May, 1929, p40), which is a somewhat romanticised ideal about children and motherhood. She said that she had "flamboyant taste in colour" (ibid), which indeed we have seen from previous examples. At one of the times when she was financially challenged, she only had one dress to wear and she describes in her autobiography how she had to wash it and then put it on wet before it had time to dry (Betty May, 2014, p192). When she was in her thirties, her sense of colour and distinctive style remained. Her lover, Jack Lindsay, recalled how she wore a "long tweed coat and a sort of robin-hood cap of green" (Lindsay, 1962, p128).

Betty May was also asked if she had been living "an immoral life" in the High Courts of Justice by Mr J.P. Eddy when she was acting as defence witness for Nina Hamnett in the Crowley libel case, her reply was: "No" (*The Times*, April 13th, 1934). Betty May also, explained to the judge that she became a "tiger woman" because she "was rather feline in looks ... I thought it was rather a good name for me" (Renninson, 2017, p104). This is a different version from earlier years when she told the popular press and whoever provided her with an audience that the reason for the name being given to her arose from her involvement with a French Apache gang.

Returning now to her birth. As we already know, she was named Bessie Golding and was born to George Golding and Ellen Theresa Golding (née James) (www.ancestry.org.uk). Bessie's father was employed as an iron-plater on ships (1891 Census) when she was born. He had various positions of employment in his lifetime, including being a gold-plater. However, in August, 1914, her father signed Attestation Papers as he had signed up for the Canadian Infantry (12th Reserve Battalion). His marital status was recorded then as widower. It is possible that his wife Ellen Golding died in approximately 1906, although strangely no death certificates are available for her, so this area of information remains a grey area about him being a widower. Just one year after signing-up to the Canadian Infantry, Private George Golding (service number 23659) died. He was buried at Tidworth Military Cemetery (www.findagrave.com/c.135) in Salisbury, Wiltshire.

Bessie Golding's paternal grandfather, Robert George Golding, was originally from Wiltshire. He had an accomplished and steady 24 year career in the London Metropolitan Police Force which started in 1866. During that time, he was promoted to sergeant in 1876, inspector in Bow in 1880, and then seventeen months later demoted to sergeant again. He finally resigned and retired from the force in 1890, the reason for leaving is unknown. However, he remained in employment, having secured a position of trust in his new job as a warehouse superintendent (www.ancestry.co.uk).

Some Ripperologists may be familiar with the name of P.C. Golding. This is because in 1888, whilst on patrol in Poplar High Street, he found the body of a lifeless woman. At first, he thought the position of her body was reminiscent of Jack the Ripper's victims. This was because the body was positioned with the left leg drawn up and the right leg stretched out, but there was no sign of injury. The body was later identified as that of Rose Mylett, a famous prostitute in the area. She was found just two miles from the centre of the Whitechapel murders and the general public's suspicion was aroused again, and inevitably the name of 'Jack the Ripper' was spoken. However, the Inquest found that Mylett died from natural causes (www.wiki.casebook.org/rose_mylett.html).

Golding resigned in April, 1890, which was well before the time that his granddaughter, Bessie, was born in 1894. Her brother, George, was born in November, 1893. In her autobiography, she claimed that she and George were sent by their mother to live with her father at a Limehouse brothel. She continued her story, claiming that her paternal grandfather had arrested her father in that brothel. The official records held by the Metropolitan Police Heritage Centre show that, when Robert George Golding retired, the account of her grandfather arresting her father, as well as her and her brother staying with their father in a brothel, was yet another fantasy, woven either by Betty May and/or George Armitage, ghostwriter of *Tiger Woman*.

Ellen Theresa Golding (née James) was Bessie's mother and her work included being a laundress and also a confectionary packer at a local factory. It may have been at one of the Frederick Allen & Sons Chocolate & Confectionary works, as the company had several chocolate factories in the East End of London (https://pasttenseblog.wordpress.com/). The 1881 Census shows an Ellen James living as a boarder with the Golding family, who were soon to become her in-laws. They were all living at 1 Brunswick Street, Poplar, and Ellen was listed as a packer in confectionery (www.ancestry.co.uk/NRO).

Bessie's maternal grandfather, John James, hailed from near Plymouth (as previously noted) and had been a labourer. He and his ancestors had been Cornish as far back as the fifteenth century. It is possible that John James came to London when the mines and tin industry were failing in Cornwall (personal communication from Black to Author). Bessie's maternal grandmother, Sarah Jane (née Abbott), hailed from Poplar (1881

Census) and in 1871 she and John James were married and living in Leicester Street, Poplar. Sadly, Sarah Jane died aged just 29 years old (www.ancestry.co.uk).

Bessie Golding's death certificate incorrectly shows her birth date as being the 5th August, 1894 (and her name is recorded as Betty MAY SEDGEWICK). Extensive research by the Author concludes that there seems to be a pattern of falsified detail and inaccurate information registered on Betty May's marriage certificates. For example, on her marriage certificate to her last husband, Noel Mostyn Sedgwick (in 1926), her father's profession was recorded as an 'artist painter' and as far as is known, he had never been a professional artist (General Records Office, marriage certificate).

But even earlier, in 1922 when she married her third husband, Frederick Charles Loveday, her father was again recorded as being a professional artist (General Records Office, marriage certificate). Previously to that, in 1916 her marriage certificate to George Gibbs King Waldron records her father (who had died the year before) as being a civil engineer. Her name is recorded as Betty Marlow Atkinson, formerly Golding (General Records Office, marriage certificate). Where the name Marlow comes from is unknown. The name Atkinson is from her first husband, Miles Linzee Atkinson, and her name is recorded as Betty Marlow Golding aged 21, when in fact she was only 20 years old.

Needless to say, researching the basic facts of Bessie Golding's life, such as her birth date, for example, has been bewildering at times. Today, providing documents and proof of identity at Registry Offices is obligatory to help stop identity fraud. During earlier times, providing evidence of identity was less strict at the Registry Offices, and so current standards will inevitably be of greater help to researchers investigating basic details, such as births, marriages and deaths.

All of her marriages were conducted in Registry Offices and had her father still been alive when she got married, perhaps he, as a follower of the Church of England faith, would have preferred her to be married in church. People have speculated that she was of Jewish heritage because then her surname Golding was a common Jewish surname, especially in the East End of London where there was a large Jewish community. However, her father and paternal grandfather are shown to be Church of England followers as shown on official records (www.ancestry.co.uk).

As previously discussed, in her 'autobiography' (first edition, 1929) she said that the contents were mainly fictional. There was also a period of her life for several years where she was missing, or perhaps even hiding from the authorities for whatever reason(s). Before the Second World War, she was known for "disappearing sometimes for weeks at a time" as her friend David Garnett remembers well (Garnett, 1955, p46). Concluding her autobiography, she procrastinated: "Sometimes I think I will leave England for a long period. It has crossed my mind to make my way to Africa – to Abyssinia, and again, I sometimes decide that I will go to Spain" (Duckworth Overlook, 2014, p222). Whether she ever went to those places is unknown to the Author.

Returning now to the article in the *Daily Express* in 1955 about Betty May having previously been missing and now being "found" – the newspaper reported that she was living in a "semi-basement bed-sitter in Luton Road, Chatham" and that after she left London she went up north.

Indeed (and as previously noted), the 1939 Register does show a 'Betty May Bailey' posing as being married to a retired fine art-dealer called H.W. Borfot Bailey (note the Register states Borfot and not Barfoot) and it mentions where they were staying, which was at the Gate House Lodge in Wirksworth, Derbyshire (Wirksworth Heritage Centre). Both of their ages were recorded as being 45 years old and, surprisingly, Betty May's birthday was entered correctly (unlike on previous documents). However, the later Electoral lists show that neither her, nor the so called 'retired art-dealer' Bailey were living at the address in Derbyshire, suggesting that it was a short-stay for them on the day the 1939 Register was compiled.

In the aforementioned newspaper article, she claimed that after the Second World War she camped out for three years on a beauty spot before she lived in the Luton Road. Why she ended up in Kent is unknown. One possible reason that she went to Kent is that she had a family connection there (a cousin once removed), a Mabel Bradley (née Walker) who, according to the 1952 Census, was living at 167 Luton Road. More than likely though, she was still with William Hubert Barfoot, as he had family connections in Folkestone, Kent. In 1957, she wrote to David Garnett from her (then) address of 23 Henry Street, Rochester, Kent. She told him that they had to vacate the condemned home and she was considering coming back to London and living in the Chalk Farm area (Northwestern University, McCormack Special Collections/Letters). It appears, however, that she never did return to North London.

Kelly's Postal Directories show Betty May Sedgwick living at 5, Skua Court in Rochester, Kent from 1965–1974 (Medway Archives), this was warden-controlled housing for the elderly. Written communication from her to David Garnett in 1977 (she was still living at the same address) shows her telling him that the warden told her that she must stop using fuel as heating and that she had to buy an electric heater. She did, and then ran up a bill of £14.38p (approximately 84 pounds today) which she could not afford to pay. She asked Garnett if he would give her some money to help pay the large bill (Northwestern University, Special Collections/Letters).

One cannot help but wonder about the authenticity of her needing money for the electricity bill, given her poor management of money. It wasn't unusual for Betty May to lie to Garnett. In his second autobiography, *Flowers of the Forest*, he described that whilst he was working as a bookseller, she sent a letter to him via an unsavoury looking character. The note said that she was ill and starving and that her landlady had taken her clothes in lieu of rent. Garnett charitably gave the man three pounds to give to Betty May. That night, Garnett went with his wife to the Café Royal, only to see Betty May at the centre of a group, the life and soul of the party. He walked up to her and said "I am glad you made such a rapid recovery ... Betty had the grace to look rather embarrassed" (Garnett, 1955, p223).

Letters exist from her to David Garnett showing that in 1957 she was living in Rochester, Kent, at 23 Henry Street (as discussed earlier) which was later demolished (Northwestern University, Special Collections/Letters). However, previously on 8th March, 1955, she wrote to him and her letter claimed that she was living at Osborne House, 26 Star Hill, Rochester, Kent (Knights, 2015, p414). This was a multi-occupied premise and records suggest that she did not live there for very long (Kent History and Library Centre – archivist). Clearly she had to move again for reasons unknown, possibly she owed rent?

In 1955, *The Daily Express* claimed that after the Second World War she camped out at a beauty spot. It is vaguely possible that she may have been living on Bluebell Hill at the time, which was the area she described to the newspaper. Bluebell Hill is a chalk hill in the county of Kent, and located between Maidstone and Rochester. It overlooks the River Medway and is part of the North Downs, it is also claimed by the locals to be haunted. Perhaps she was homeless at this time and not "camping out" as she had told the newspaper.

However, an acquaintance who knew Betty May in the early 1970's recalled what Betty May told her: "At one time she lived in a tent or something on the Bluebell Hill in Kent, as her partner (who remained unnamed but who probably was Hubert William Barfoot, aka 'Billy') had tuberculosis and needed constant fresh air" (communication from Jane Dalley to Author). Interestingly, Hubert William Barfoot's father also lived in Kent in the early 1940's, and he died in Folkestone on 27th May, 1942 (www.ancestry.org.uk/NRO). Betty May remained in Kent as Betty May Sedgewick until her death on 5th May, 1980, where she died in the Medway Hospital in Gillingham (she used an extra 'e' in her married surname 'Sedgwick', the reason unknown). She had been taken to the hospital from her flat at 5 Skua Court, Bligh Way, Strood in Rochester, Kent.

Virginia Nicholson summed up Betty May's last few years, and wrote that she was reduced to living in council housing in the 1970's and that "Betty eked out her last years living on handouts from the state, and a small stipend from her one-time lover, and memories" (Nicholson, 2002, p290). The one-time lover referred to here is Nicholson's relation, David Garnett. He was an unsung hero in Betty May's life, having known her since she was a teenager and being of financial support to her throughout her life. He was a generous and kind person and even set up a modest trust fund for her. His charitable nature is further indicated by him also setting up trust funds for two farm-workers who used to work on his farm for him (Knights, 2015, p479).

Betty May's death certificate states that she died from 'pulmonary embolism', 'cardiac arrhythmia' and 'atherosclotic heart disease' (General Records Office/Death Certificate). This tells us that she had blood clots on the lungs, her heart was not working properly and that she had hardening and plaque inside her arteries. She had a Public Health Funeral (aka pauper's funeral) and her ashes buried in the plot 276 in an unmarked spot in Strood Cemetery in Cuxton Road, Kent (Kent Library & History Centre).

When and why exactly Bessie Golding changed her name to 'Betty May', we do not know. Although, it is probable that she used it as her professional name for modelling. She appears never to have returned to using her given name 'Bessie Golding'. Perhaps she wanted to reinvent herself and forget the life into which she was born, as well as escaping from any situations where she didn't want to be found later on.

Bessie Golding who was raised in the slums of East End London and who died in Kent led a life punctuated by adventure, fantasy, gaiety and unpredictability, fused with dependency, loss and sadness. She used her 'street-nous' and instincts, living on her wits, having adopted a fatalistic and sometimes irresponsible attitude about life. In her earlier and final years, she lived sparsely but nonetheless retained her grittiness, humour and strong survival instincts.

When she was married to Raoul Loveday, Aleister Crowley claimed when the Loveday's were living in one room in Fitzroy Street that it was a "foul, frowsty, venomous den ... they were living from hand to mouth" (Crowley, 1979, p905). On another occasion, she was forced to sell her wedding ring from Loveday because when they were on the final part of their travels to visit Crowley at his Abbey in Cefalu, they had insufficient money to pay for the last train fare from Palermo to Cefalu (Betty May, 2014, p153). Much to her infuriation, she had to sacrifice her wedding ring for that journey.

When she and her partner Edgell Rickword (an editor, communist and poet) were living in Maidenhead in 1932, they were living from his Disability Pension; this was approximately £3 and 10 shillings. Rickword had his left eye removed in 1919 as it had become badly infected with general septicaemia). These examples show how she was living without luxury and living simply on the bare essentials.

Letters from Betty May to David Garnett from the 1950's through to her final years suggest that she *may* not have been financially supported by Hubert William Barfoot, hence her consistent requests to Garnett for money (Northwestern University, Special Collections/Letters). It is difficult to know for certain what is fact and what is fiction where Betty May is concerned, especially when it comes to financial matters. Sadly for her, Hubert William Barfoot never changed his will, which was made in 1935 (ibid). If he had, it would have ensured that Betty May would be financially supported after his death or would inherit anything else from his estate. Instead, Barfoot's pension went to his wife, Agnes (née Hart), whom he never divorced (Ministry of Pensions and National Insurance card). Once again, Betty May was omitted from any financial security agreement even though she had cohabited with him and apparently cared for him over a long period of time.

At the end of her autobiography (which covers approximately her first 30 years) she said: "I am sure that I am born for adventure" (Duckworth Overlook, 2014, p222), showing that she was expecting to still live a life of escapade, and probably notoriety. Her autobiography concludes: "One of these days you will certainly hear of me again, and perhaps read of the further adventures of Betty May" (ibid), and indeed she was later to be heard of again ... as you can see in reading this chapter.

PART 3: ASTROLOGY IN ACTION

For continuity purposes, Bessie Golding will now be referred to as Betty May.

When Betty May was born on 25th August, 1894, the outer planets were in the following positions: Saturn in Libra, Uranus in Scorpio, and Neptune and Pluto in Gemini. The latter planets in Gemini represent a generation of people; this is because the planets remain in those signs for a long period of time; Neptune for fourteen years and Pluto for thirty years. Pluto has an ecliptical orbit so is not always thirty years in a sign, but it was when Betty May was born and it spanned from 1884 to 1919.

THE INFLUENCE OF THE OUTER PLANETS ON BETTY MAY'S GENERTION

Betty May lived until she was 85 and during that time she moved from one social class to another, she lived through four sovereigns on the throne and survived the two World Wars. The world had changed significantly since Betty May was born in 1894. The period of change in which she lived was an erratic and intense time; people were determined, strong-willed (Uranus in Scorpio) and survived two World Wars. The transformation that the wars brought included thousands of deaths and indeed hers was a generation where death was all around them and life would never be the same again.

Saturn was in Libra between 1892 and 1923, and when Betty May was born; Saturn had already been in Libra for two years. During this cycle, some of the key events that happened in this Saturn in Libra generation were the following: The Education Act of 1918 came into law and raised the school leaving age from twelve to fourteen. It abolished all fees in state elementary schools and widened the provision of medical inspection, nursery schools and special-needs education. In 1923, the Matrimonial Causes Act established equal rights in divorce for men and women. This made it possible for wives to divorce their husbands for adultery; previously they had been unable to. Also in 1923, The Liquor Act came into being which made it illegal to sell alcohol to people under eighteen in England, clearly society was changing.

Addressing the Neptune in Gemini position now. One way it may be manifested can be seen by some of the narrow-mindedness of the Victorian era. People may have 'wanted to believe what they wanted to believe' perhaps unable and unwilling to differentiate fact from fiction. One example of this can be seen through Queen Victoria's belief that only men participated in same-sex relationships and would be treated as criminals and prosecuted for this. Neptune in Gemini also suggests that it was a period where gossip and scandal was rife. One example of this can be seen in the East End of London where rumours flourished about the Whitechapel Murders, which soon became known as the 'Jack the Ripper Murders.' Even today, there remains uncertainty and mystery about who 'Jack the Ripper' was, as he was never caught. Some people believe the murders were the savage work of more than one person. His legacy remains to this day and there are even Jack the Ripper tours and walks. The ambiguity and uncertainty in this example about who committed these murders correspond with Neptune, whilst the gossip and tittle-tattle are connected with the communication side of Gemini.

Potentially, if one was the subject of gossip and tittle-tattle, it could lead to their undoing, one example being loss of employment. Betty May, as we already know, became the subject of scandal in her earlier days. One example of this is shown by her appearing in the tabloid newspapers. The conjunction between Neptune and Pluto in Gemini at the time she was born; this is an indicator from that time of the significant levels of crime, prostitution and violence in deprived neighbourhoods. Rarely was this vicious cycle broken in poverty-stricken communities.

The Pluto in Gemini stirred a generation that was curious and transforming. The world that Betty May knew as a child had changed forever as she grew into a young adult. Two examples of major transformations in the Pluto in Gemini generation include: the invention of powered flight in 1903 and the birth of the Labour Party in 1900. The aforementioned outer planets (Uranus, Neptune and Pluto) will be discussed on a more personal level further on.

OBTAINING HER TIME OF BIRTH

Betty May was born under the sign of Virgo on the 25th August, 1894, in Canning Town, West Ham, England (G.R.O. birth certificate). Her time of birth is unknown, however it can be ascertained using a system called 'rectification'. This involves looking at significant events in her life and calculating the transiting outer planets in her natal chart and interpreting any aspects. From the process of rectification, a birth time of 1:00am has been concluded for Betty May. This involved looking at the dates of her marriages, her admission and discharge from institutions, a day she was in court giving evidence as a defence witness, the date of her father's death as well as the date of her own death. It is interesting that her time of birth has been calculated as 1:00am, as Betty May told a pub friend that "she loved the nightlife" (correspondence from Jane Dalley to Author) and, as we know, Betty May thrived when she was clubbing, drinking and performing through to the early hours of the following day.

INTERPRETING BETTY MAY'S NATAL CHART

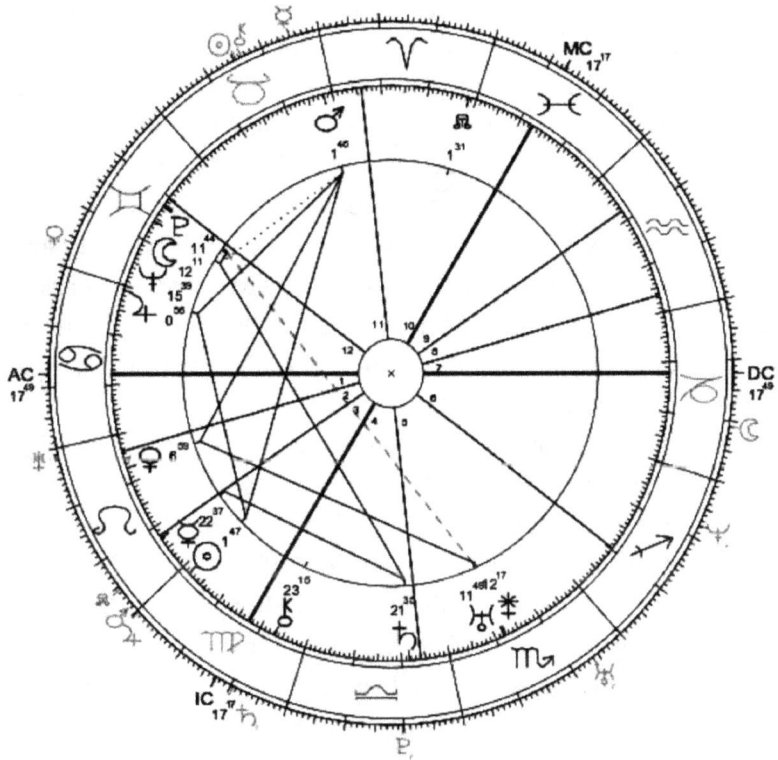

Rectified natal and transits chart for the day that Betty May died on 5th May, 1980

There are three positions in her natal chart which are significant as they are the native positions in the natural zodiac (*see glossary*), they are: Venus in the second house, Mercury in the third house, and Neptune in the twelfth house. This means that the planets' energy in these houses are particularly strong, each of these positions will be discussed further on in more detail.

The air element is also emphasised in the natal chart, which comprises of: Moon, Neptune and Pluto in Gemini; as well as Saturn in Libra. The strong presence of the air element in the chart reveals that Betty May was curious, ideas-orientated and sociable but at times could lack in empathy and even seem indifferent to others. An example of her coldness and insensitivity can be seen by the following situation: when she and Loveday were staying with Crowley and some of his other disciples at the Abbey of Thelema in Sicily in 1923, a scene ensued and was described by Leah Hirsig. In her statement about the event, she was part of the Thelemite group and played the role of the Scarlet Woman. She wrote that Betty May was "rude, insolent and thoroughly unfit to be in a room where her sick husband lay" (www.100thmonkeypress.com). Betty May had been asked several times by Crowley not to read the daily newspapers, as it was forbidden for her to do so at the temple. However, she refused and insisted on reading them.

When she was asked a final time not to read them she went berserk and became violent, in the sick-room where her husband lay seriously ill. Crowley had entered the room to speak with her about her defiance and to coax her out of the room where her ill husband lay. It was at this point that Hirsig suddenly "heard the smashing of glass and knocking about of chairs etc. She had suddenly started to scream and swear and to throw jugs etc at the K.G.S.L. (Knight Guardian of the Sacred Lance – Crowley)" (ibid).

Upon hearing the commotion, Leah had entered into Mr and Mrs Loveday's room where there "was a lighted oil lamp in the room, also an oil stove" (ibid). Hirsig found Betty May kicking Crowley "who was holding her – she being in violent hysterics" (ibid). There were smashed bottles and glass on her husband's sickbed and Loveday had gotten out of his bed barely able to stand (ibid). Betty May's parting words to her sick husband were coldly delivered without any thought for his health and she demanded of him: "Goodbye Raoul, send down my passport to-morrow" (ibid). This situation shows her lack of regard for her husband's ill-health and her cold and aggressive nature. We will see further on other examples of her violent and hot temper.

Returning again to the astrology, there is also an emphasis on the positive polarity (*see glossary*) in her natal chart, which indicates that Betty May was assertive, courageous and extrovert. This energy is seen by the aforementioned planets in Gemini and Libra, as well as Mercury and Venus in Leo (to be discussed further on). There is a balanced energy of the fixed and mutable modes (*see glossary*) which shows that Betty May could be determined and obstinate, but was also able to recognise when she needed to be flexible. This mutable energy would have helped prevent her from becoming too set in her ways and to move on, both physically and mentally.

MERCURY, WINGED MESSENGER, PRANKSTER AND TRICKSTER

The rectified natal chart shows that the Sun was in Virgo at one degree and the Moon was in Gemini at twelve degrees when Betty May was born. Both of these signs are ruled by Mercury but have different characteristics in each of the signs. Virgo is an earth sign and belongs to the mutable mode and feminine polarity whilst Gemini is an air sign and also belongs to the mutable mode but the masculine polarity (*see glossary for explanation these terms*).

This astrological data suggests that Betty May was discerning and resourceful, had a quick and agile mind and a nervous energy which may have manifested in stress and tensions, making relaxation difficult for her, she remarked that she had a touchy

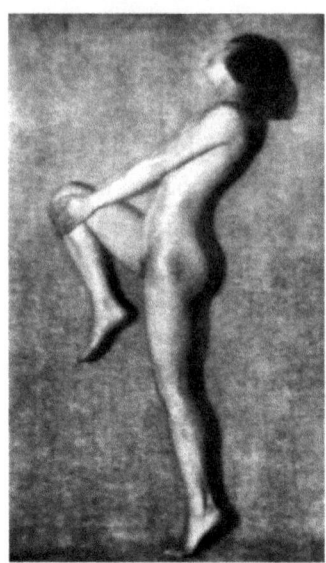

BM in Bas Relief Pose by Angus Basil. British Newspaper Archive from *The Sketch*, approx.1924.

condition of her nerves (Betty May, 2014, p210). The Sun is positioned in the third house and emphasises that she had a thirst for knowledge and was keen to be seen as clever, as well as indicating that she spoke from the heart and was a natural communicator. Virgo is seen as a goddess or virgin, holding a corn sheaf which represents the harvest, and its associations include fertility and usefulness. Authors; Lindsay River and Sally Gillespie wrote that in ancient times, the word 'virgin' did not mean celibacy as it does in contemporary times, but instead "was a woman who belonged to no man, who was her own mistress, aware of her powers and value. She formed relationships and made love when she chose to, but never gave up her right to self-determination" (River & Gillespie, 1987, p165). This definition is certainly borne out by the lifestyle of Betty May, as we have already seen, and indeed by the way others saw her. She was fiercely independent and loved to love and loved to make love. Atkins recalled from what Betty May confided in her that "she seemed to go through men very quickly" (personal correspondence from Ian Black to Author).

Mercury is in the third house and is at home here in the natural zodiac (*see glossary*). This position repeats the theme of her having an agile and restless mind, of being very curious and observant, as well as being quick-witted, a jester and storyteller but she also could be deceitful and wily. Her friend, Nina Hamnett, said in her first autobiography that whilst there was a vivid description about life in Cefalù, the version "was not half so good

BETTY MAY (1894–1980)

as the way in which she told me the story herself" (Hamnett, 1984, p176). There is a sextile aspect created between Mercury and Saturn, which suggests that she had a caustic sense of humour. This is because Mercury is associated with humour and Saturn is associated with 'dryness', it also suggests 'straight-talking' and that she could 'tell it as it was,' speaking directly and to the point. Indeed, author and journalist, W.B. Seabrook, recalled that when he interviewed her in August, 1928, that she told her story using "straightforward phrases ... it

By Ashley Basil, CC=BY 2.0.

was an amazingly outspoken account, from which nothing was withheld" (*Evansville Courier* – Seabrook, 1928, page unknown). This shows how straightforward and direct she could be at times but, as we shall learn further on, when it came to guarding and defending her privacy, she could be equally as defensive and digress from areas of her life she did not wish to discuss.

Sagittarius on the sixth house cusp also shows that Betty May sought mental stimulation in her daily life, and routines that were needed may have been strewn rather than carefully planned. Certainly, any work that was confining and monotonous would have bored and discouraged her. For example, when she was a teenager working as a domestic servant, this employment did not last for very long, although the reasons why for that are unknown. Excess is an association of Sagittarius (and its ruler, Jupiter) and it indicates that overdoing things could underline some health issues. This theme is further emphasised by Jupiter being present in the twelfth house and was pertinent to Betty May in terms of her alcohol and drug addiction.

Areas of work that held an element of adventure or taking a gamble would have been more appealing to her, as these are associations of Sagittarius. This can be seen through her photography modelling for Angus Basil, where she posed artistically nude for him. One example of this is seen by a graceful and lithe photograph called *'Bas Relief'* (*The Sketch*, 1924, page number unknown). At such times, women were considered immoral for posing nude, and considered scandalous by society. Betty May not only posed nude for him but also modelled some of the latest fashions of the day, including trendy black hats.

HUMOUR, WIT AND YOUTHFULNESS

The Moon in Gemini shows she had a mental approach to emotional issues and it also indicates that she could be flighty and restless, mercurial and temperamental. Alongside that, the Moon in Gemini shows that information exchange, gossip and social interaction were important to her, satisfying her thirst for communication and knowledge. She could be light-hearted, humorous and witty, as these are correspondences of Mercury, the ruler of Gemini (and Virgo). As previously noted, Hugh David recalled in his book, *The Fitzrovians*, how Betty May shrieked with laughter as she, Lillian Shelley and sometimes Nina Hamnett sung their way through raucous folk songs (David, 1988, p118). David Garnett described Betty May in her early twenties as having "a great sense of humour as well as extraordinary vitality" (Garnett, 1955, p46). Even when they met up again in the mid-1950's, when she would have been approximately 61 years old, he described her as "most charming; not much changed – white hair, very alive" (Knights, 2015, p414).

In her later years, she still enjoyed light-hearted and youthful company, which would have suited her Moon in Gemini. For example, in approximately 1965, when she would have been around 70 years old, she drank in The Queen Charlotte pub in

Rochester, Kent. Patrons recalled how "she would hold court with a group of teenagers who were interested in art and music ... she mainly spoke with the females." She never drank alone and "would always be holding court ... she was quite grand but not snobbish" (correspondence from Bernard Cherry to Author). With pride, she told her enthusiastic and interested teenaged audience how she used to be a model for Epstein and Kramer. Customers from another pub in Kent recall how she drank in a pub that had a mainly young clientele, and how she loved the young people and enjoyed the youthful environment (personal correspondence from Ben Levy to Author). This shows how, even though she was in her seventies, she was exuberant and young at heart still, refused to be labelled and also had the mental capacity to be able to easily communicate and mix with teenagers.

MAGIC AND THE MOON

Betty May was born on a waning quarter Moon and astrologer and author, Raven Kaldera, identified that this Moon, when it is in Gemini, is known as the 'Magician's Moon'. This is pertinent to Betty May, as not only did she have knowledge of magic herself but aparently she first met ceremonial magician, Aleister Crowley, in the Cafe Royal in 1914. Later (and as already discussed), her third husband, Frederick Charles Loveday, became a disciple of Crowley and his magic. Kaldera observed that people born under a Magician's Moon "continually fight against the urge to manipulate others" (Kaldera, 2011, p281) and play with their emotions, and indeed this is in keeping with Mercury, in the sense that Mercury's associations include changeability – it can be a trickster at times as well as a 'messenger' (amongst other things!).

Kaldera also observed that 'Magician Moon' people "battle a general distrust of people ... they tend to want secrecy and prefer to withhold information, for reasons of keeping power to themselves" (ibid). An example of her need for privacy can be seen whereby a female pub contact of hers observed that (when Betty May was in her seventies) "she kept everything to herself, very private and only told you something real personal if she wanted you to know" (personal correspondence to Author from Levy). One way that Betty May was only too eager to learn about others was by insisting that she read their palms. The same person said that she "oozed some kind of power" and that there was "something chilling about her" (ibid). Astrological data in her natal chart backs this up, for the Moon, Neptune and Pluto are in the twelfth house – the area of elusiveness and secrets. The Moon is the ruler of her natal chart because the ascendant is Cancer which is ruled by the Moon, and so makes it very important in the natal chart. The Moon conjunct Neptune and Pluto will be discussed further on in more detail.

CHART SHAPE

There is a chart shape in Betty May's natal chart which is called 'The Bowl' – half the chart has planets in it, but the other half is empty (Uranus is just 10 degrees beyond the occupied half). The chart shape can suggest several possibilities; one being that she sought self-improvement and was critical of not only herself but others also (which are also themes associated with Virgos). In a way, she could be described as 'a work in progress' which is befitting to the artist's model and sitter that Betty May was. The 'Bowl' chart shape also suggests that she may have always been searching to meet her 'other half' to make herself feel complete and validated; this could be a partnership in either a business or personal sense. The latter was certainly borne out in Betty May's life, particularly in personal relationships, as will be discussed further on.

The symbolism also suggests that she was a 'one-sided' individual, in that she had tremendous self-interest, which is shown also by the Sun trine Mars aspect in her natal chart and at times she may even have shown total disregard for other people and their feelings. One example of this can be seen whereby when she was a lover of Jack Lindsay, both of them were friends with editor and poet, Edgell Rickword (in 1930 he became an active Communist). He was a published war poet and, interestingly, wrote a poem called, *The Lousy Astrologer's Present to his Sweetheart* (Rickword, 1976, p102), which is believed to be dedicated to Betty May (personal correspondence to Author from Publisher).

Betty May asked Lindsay, "Do you mind if I go and live with Edgell? Do you say I mustn't?" (Lindsay, 1962, p140). Lindsay was startled by her question, more so because he had never noticed that Rickword was especially interested in her (ibid). However, Lindsay was pleased to let her go and have her freedom and the three of them remained friends, but Betty May and Edgell Rickword began a three-year affair. They lived in Maidenhead in Berkshire, had a cottage in the south of England, and also lived in different parts of London; the affair amicably fizzled out in approximately 1933. Then Betty May went to live with author, Communist and poet, Hugh Sykes Davies, in South Hill Park, Hampstead, London.

COURAGE, STRENGTH AND RISK-TAKING

Returning again to Betty May's natal astrology, the Sun and Mars contact indicates that she had tremendous courage and strength, at times she could be impatient and impulsive, perhaps making errors in her haste, going in head-first without any thought for the consequences. Lindsay said of her that she "took what she wanted instead of being taken, resolute mistress of herself instead of being a victim" (Lindsay, 1962, p129). This shows the assertive and independent nature of her, as well as a preparation for being 'nobody's fool'. Astrologer and author, Sue Tompkins, observed that people with the Sun trine Mars in their natal chart may not only live out the courageous and daring side of their nature but are also attracted to partners who are similar to them, in that they take action, are capable of taking risks and have a pioneering spirit about them; which is in keeping with characteristics of Mars (Tompkins, 1990, p104).

This is borne out by at least two of Betty May's husbands being in the military (a Mars association), as well as having relationships with the aforementioned poets who became Communists (Edgell Rickword and Hugh Sykes Davies). She also lived in a commune-come-squat for artists and creatives in Osmond Terrace in North-West London which was set-up by pioneer, Stewart Gray. He was a campaigner who fought against poverty and unemployment in the early 1900's and he was also the originator of the 'Back-to-the-Land' movement in the United Kingdom. This movement called for people to become more self-sufficient and grow their own food on a small plot of land and adopt a greater sense of community. Her fourth husband, Noel Mostyn Sedgwick, also was mutinous, in that he did not follow the previous three generations of clergy in his family: his father, grandfather and great-grandfather were all clergymen (www.ancestry.co.uk). Sedgwick's father died when he was fourteen and he carved out his own career and became a sporting editor and distinguished author.

The Sun trine Mars aspect also suggests that Betty May was a born fighter who dared to take risks and liked to find new areas to conquer. Certainly, in her determination to break away from her class and family and the hardworking and impoverished life into which she was born. She rebelled against previous working-class generations in her family, entering into circles of bohemianism, became a creative and married into wealthier families than her own, where she was not expected to work. This was in contrast to her mother, for example, who had worked long and hard hours for a pittance of a wage (e.g. a packer in a confectionary factory). She worked a twelve-hour day in order to bring home a weekly income of ten shillings a week (Betty May, 2014, p14). Edgell Rickwood described Betty May as being a "forceful personality in violent revolt against society" (Hobday, 1989, p268).

Another example of her risk-taking nature is recalled by David Garnett whereby in the mid-1930's she appeared in Court on a charge of insulting behaviour (Garnett, 1955, p224). A very handsome young police officer had been on duty at the junction of Goodge Street and the Tottenham Court Road. Betty May went up to him, put her arms around him and kissed him repeatedly (ibid). The judge asked her what she had to say in her defence, in her most demure voice she replied: "Well, your worship, just look at him, he's so handsome ... I could not help it." She was fortunate, she was bound over not to kiss any more policeman who were on duty and discharged (ibid).

Because Mars is connected with anger, conflict and violence (amongst other things!), it is unsurprising that she became notorious for her brawling and rages, something she was unashamedly proud of. One example of this is as follows: on Armistice Day, 1918, artist and author, C.N.W. Nevison, recalls in his memoirs how on that evening he and his wife Katherine were attending a party in Regent's Park. However, in the early hours they decided to leave as "Betty May suddenly armed herself with fire-irons and tried to start a new war" (Nevison, 1938, pp112,113), which was dangerous to say the least. Dolores (a friend of Betty May who was also an artist's model) said of her that, she "was fierce and sinuous as the animal whose name she adopted" (*Pittsburgh Sun. Telegraph*, Dolores, 1930, page number unknown). When she was in her thirties, she threw a cup of tea in Mrs Segwick's (her mother-in-law's) face,

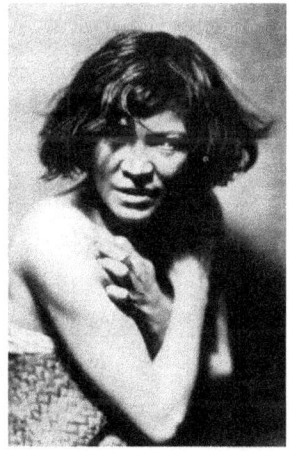

'Betty May' by Ashley Basil.
CC by 2.0

and the cup shattered into tiny pieces on the floor. Betty May was ill and irritated by her mother-in-law's constant attention and fussing (Betty May, 2014, p212). She later elaborated that "it was with the greatest difficulty that I refrained from slapping her face" (ibid), clearly she had no patience or respect for Mrs Sedgwick, putting it mildly. However, she was less violent in her older age and in her own words in a letter to Garnett wrote: "there comes a time in one's life when one has to slow down" (Betty May to Garnett, approx. Dec, 1972). She was 78 at this time. Pub friends from Kent recalled how she "usually had rows with men and had the last word … she could put you down with words and she did not have to shout" (personal correspondence from Levy to Author).

Mars is positioned in the eleventh house – the area associated with clubs, kindred spirits, friends and groups. Her competitive spirit is likely to have been stimulated in groups and she could have also been assertive and inspired. However, this position indicates that she could have had quarrelsome relationships with friends and been unreasonably demanding, thus creating conflicts. This is because those areas are also associated with Mars. The other angle with Mars in the eleventh house is that she could have been inspiring to her friends and led the way in areas where others may not. One example of this can be seen by her highly spirited nature with a self-determination to do things how and when she wanted.

The Sun in Virgo and Mars in Taurus in her natal chart shows that she could be practical and liked to be active and vigorous. She needed to channel her energy and be productive, the danger being that if she didn't, she would become bored and destructive. Both Virgo and Taurus are ruled by the earth element which is associated with productivity and usefulness. The former sign is known for having a bright mind and resourcefulness and the latter sign for its determination, earthiness and sensuality.

BETTY MAY (1894–1980)

OPPORTUNITIES AND SEXUAL ADVENTURES

Mars is sextile Jupiter in her natal chart and indicates her tremendous physical strength as well as great optimism. David Garnett recalled how "in every look and gesture she revealed the toughness and independence that one sees in the women who work in circuses and travelling shows" (Garnett, 1955, 44). Mars sextile Jupiter also suggests that she had opportunities to help her achieve her ambition; for example, becoming a model and that she also had the determination and vision to ensure that it happened. Another interpretation of this aspect is that it points to her many sexual adventures, since Mars is associated with the former and Jupiter the latter. Interestingly, her husbands were Sun signs which fall into the cardinal mode (*see glossary*), these were: Miles Linzee Atkinson a Cancer, George Dibbs King Waldron an Aries, Raoul (Frederick Charles) Loveday also a Cancer and Noel Mostyn Sedgwick a Capricorn. The cardinal signs (which also include Libra) show that she was attracted to people who were assertive and challenging.

As we already know, Betty May also co-habited with William Hubert Barfoot (a Libra), this lasting (as far as we know) from approximately 1937 right through to his death in 1963 and, if this is correct, it was the longest period of time she had stayed with a husband/partner. Whether she was faithful during this partnership, we do not know. What is certain is that she got bored very quickly and monogamy did not come easily to her, as previous relationships indicate. However, she was indeed a magnet to men who were equally as individual and daring as she was. One other example of this (aside from Barfoot) is the aforementioned Hyman Coutts.

APPEARANCES AND ATTRACTION

Betty May's ascendant (*see glossary*) sign was Cancer, which is ruled by the Moon, as previously noted – just as the Moon's energy waxes and wanes, so did Betty May's moods. Certainly, she could be amicable and sociable, but she was also changeable and moody. The ascendant is also an indication of one's appearance and first impressions. She was so tiny that she told the readers of her autobiography that she was no more than five feet in height (Betty May, 2014, p14) and took a tiny size 1 in shoe size (ibid, p94). Because she was so small and almost childlike in appearance, this may have stirred feelings in others whereby they wanted to care for and protect her, which are qualities associated with Cancer and the Moon. However, woe betide the person who thought that Betty May needed looking after or saving, as they soon found out that she was a mighty force of independence.

Cancer also shows that she was exceptionally intuitive and perceptive and could keep concealed her true emotions and feelings when she wanted to as a form of protection, just as a Crab (the symbol of Cancer) is able to protect itself. The Moon is positioned in the twelfth house in her natal chart and further emphasises that she hid her true feelings and at times needed privacy and introspection, thus emphasising again the theme of protecting her true emotions and feelings. The Moon in this house also shows that she was artistic, imaginative and psychic. The Cancer ascendant also indicates that she could be sentimental and romantic about the past. One example of this can be seen whereby she regularly spoke about her modelling days and the artists that she sat for, even though her career in that area was short-lived.

CARE AND SECURITY

The Capricorn descendant shows that she was attracted to people who could have offered her the reliability and financial security that she may have been seeking and, indeed, three of her husbands were able to offer her that assurance. However, the business of marriage was unsuited to her free-spirited and liberated personality, monogamy did not suit her and she threw away opportunities of potentially being secure in the tradition of marriage, finding it confining and limited.

Saturn, the ruler of Capricorn, is resident in the fourth house in Betty May's natal chart. This is the area that is associated with family, heritage and roots. It is also associated with a caretaking figure: traditionally it is the mother, although in modern times the caretaker can be indicative of either mother/father or other care-giver. We know that Betty May had a variety of 'care-givers', from her paternal grandparents to her great aunt and great uncle, and they may have been disciplinarians and strict with Betty May, since these are associations of Saturn. Positioned in the fourth house, Saturn also signifies that she came from a hard-working and respected family. However, there were likely to have been conditions of emotional coldness and an authority figure that was unable to show affection and love, these are also Saturn associations. The energy of Saturn also suggests that she may have become self-sufficient very early on in childhood. At times, she may have felt frustrated and isolated, as these are both characteristics of Saturn.

This was certainly borne out in Betty May's life when she was a young child, as we have seen from previous illustrations about her background and childhood, as well as some of her stories in *Tiger Woman, My Story*. Saturn in the fourth house also suggests that she found it difficult to put roots down and find a solid base in home life. This is because the fourth house is associated with domesticity and roots, whilst Saturn corresponds with challenges and obstacles. Areas such as duties and obstructions, diligence and rules are other associations of Saturn which shows austerity and bleakness in her early life. One example of this can be seen when she was employed as a general domestic servant when she was a teenager on the aforementioned farm in Surrey. The duties and responsibilities involved, plus an early start to the working day and long hours of manual work was probably unsuitable to her unpredictable nature, perhaps this is why she did not remain in employment at the farm for very long.

A THIRST FOR KNOWLEDGE AND LEARNING LINES

Mercury is sextile Saturn and suggests that she may have come from a background where there were no books or reading materials and where there was little room for conversation or learning. Therefore, it must have satisfied her thirst for knowledge when she went to school, where her agile and curious mind could receive at least some mental stimulation. No doubt, though, the discipline and routine of school-life would have become a bore to her eventually. When she was an adult, she enjoyed reading and liked authors such as Edgar Wallace (Betty May, 1929, p210) and H.E. Bates (Northwestern University/Letter, May 1957). She read *The Sunday Times* (Northwestern University Special Collections/Letters) and was also a member of her local library in Kent (ibid). When she was an adult, she was drawn to people who held careers associated with Mercury, such as editors and reporters, journalists and writers.

The aforementioned aspect between Mercury and Saturn may have helped her learn the words to songs too, and it may have been a natural ability for her since the sextile (*see glossary*) is a soft aspect (ibid). Her repertoire included the traditional folksong, *Those Raggle Taggle Gypsies*; Scottish ballad, *The Bonnie Earl O' Moray;* and from Shakespeare's *Much Ado about Nothing*, the verse *Sigh No More Ladies;* and the sea-shanty, *The Maid from Amsterdam*. She was known for especially singing these songs at The Cave of The Golden Calf night club in central London. Author, Arthur Calder-Marshall, wrote that the quiet of his street broken by "a rather nice voice singing *The Raggle-Taggle Gypsies*" (Calder-Marshall, 1990, p101), that voice belonged to Betty May.

The nightclub was set up in 1912 for the aristocratic classes and Bohemian artists, by Frida Strindberg (by then the ex-wife of playwright, Augustus Strindberg). Her enterprise was short-lived, lasting approximately two years. Apparently, as time went on in the evening the atmosphere became more frantic and the tempo quickened, which in turn led to the gypsy orchestra becoming impassioned and led by a frenzied Hungarian fiddler (Hooker, 1986, p47). Betty May also worked at the Crab Tree Club in Soho, London, which was established in 1914 by painter, Augustus John. There Betty May was the principal support for the music hall entertainer Lillian Shelley who sang *Popsy Wopsy* and *You Made Me Love You* (Hamnett, 1984, p47). British surrealist painter and war artist, Paul Nash, revealed his disdain for the venue and called it "a most disgusting place! A place of utter coarseness" (https://en.wikipedia.org).

ORDER, HYGIENE AND PRACTICALITIES

Virgo is the sign on the IC (*see glossary*) and suggests that Betty May moved home several times. This is because Mercury the ruler of Virgo (and Gemini) is associated with adaptability, movement and agility. Indeed, we have seen how many times she moved homes in her life for varying reasons. Cleanliness, hygiene and a neat environment are also associated with Virgo and this may have made her feel more grounded and secure if she had this in her home environment. Virgo on the IC also shows that she could be practical, resourceful and skillful when she wanted to be.

Her home-help, Eleanore Atkins, recalled that Betty May's flat in Skua Court in Kent "was kept spotless and she did most of it herself" (personal correspondence from Black to Author). This shows that not only was this important to Betty May but also how physically sprightly she still was at that time. Atkins observed of her during that period that although she had no money "she had nice clothes … and took pride in her appearance and cleanliness" (ibid). Cleanliness and hygiene may have been important to her, as she remembered what it was like growing up in the East End where disease was rife and there was poor sanitation, so keeping one's home clean was a priority for health reasons. Betty May recalled how her mother "persevered in keeping us and our home clean" (Betty May, 2014, p14). She continued that her mother was unable to catch the black-beetles, and Betty May remembered "the sensation of crushing them under my bare feet. They used to give a sort of scrunch" (ibid).

When Jack Lindsay went to visit her and Rickword in their cottage in the south of England (possibly Lewes or Kent), he described her in the following way: "Betty looked so like a hardworking gypsy in the rough conditions … Betty flinging back the hair from her sweaty face, bares her house-wifely elbows" (Lindsay, 1962, p155). Author, Virginia Nicholson wrote that: "Betty May spent a brief period playing house with one of her many husbands, rearranging the furniture and whitewashing the walls, but before long it was back to Bohemia: the pleasures of housekeeping grew stale as fast as the other pleasures of this provoking world" (Nicholson, 2002, p217). Such mundane chores may have been necessary but with Mercury ruling her Sun and Moon sign, Betty May would always need stimulus and a variety of people around her, to satisfy her intellectual self, where conversation, exchange of ideas and excitement could take place.

When she was staying at the Abbey of Thelema with her husband and Crowley, she didn't enjoy life there; finding it dirty and she could not get on with Crowley or Ninette Shumway (http://www.elisarolle.com). Betty May complained about Shumway that, she was "slovenly in her ways" and that she "could not work with her" (www.100thmonkeypress.com Leah Hirsig, 12th Feb, 1923).

This shows the critical and discerning nature of the Virgo IC and given that Betty May and Ninette Shumway both worked in the kitchen at the Abbey; it would have been frustrating to Betty May not to see cleanliness, hygiene and organisation in place. It also shows that when Betty May worked, she wanted to work to the best of her ability and expected the same standards from her co-workers.

Chiron the Wounded Healer (*see glossary*) is also in Virgo and in the fourth house. Astrologer and author, Melanie Reinhart, observed that for some people with Chiron in Virgo control is often an issue – either too much or too little of it. Certainly being able to control her temper had been an issue in Betty May's life, even in her later years she said that she was having problems still with her hot- temper (Northwestern University/Letter, 1972) and managing her money also seemed to have remained an issue. Reinhart also recognised that those with Chiron in Virgo may feel that they have to constantly organise their thoughts to ward off the pandemonium that always seems to be nearby (Reinhart, 1989, p132). She also observed that some people could be chaotic and disorganised as well as very mediumistic (ibid, p133) and all of these areas were especially pertinent to Betty May.

Furthermore, Chiron in the fourth house is observed by Reinhart as being an indication that the Chiron 'wound' is connected with early mothering and essential security needs and that people with this placement in their natal chart yearn for a home, belonging and security (ibid, p122). Certainly, this is an area that Betty May constantly strived for throughout her life and the constant upheaval of moving home and being unable to put down roots throughout her life must have added to her anxious and nervous energy. In her later life, she was able at least to secure a local authority flat for several years. Before she was awarded her council flat, she was constantly moving from one private accommodation home to another, which must have exacerbated insecurities she may have had.

AMPLIFICATION, BELIEF AND FUTURISM

The Sun is sextile Jupiter in Betty May's chart and adds to the theme of belief in one's self, the desire to take risks and also to take a gamble in life. This aspect would also include expanding one's horizons, as well as looking on the bright side of life, even when there have been hard knocks in life, and with a view that the grass is always greener on the other side. This is also a good aspect for self-promotion, which Betty May readily undertook, one example being her frequently going to the newspapers with a story for a 'quick buck', whether it was true or not.

There is also a tendency, with the Sun and Jupiter aspect to over-extend oneself, as well as being prone to exaggeration; this is seen through qualities of Jupiter which include abundance and embellishment. Other correspondences of the planet include beliefs, philosophy, religion and travel, as well as having a concern with the future and looking at the broader picture of life. No doubt this would have been helpful to her when she was predicting future outcomes for herself and other people – the latter, for example, through her ability to read palms and tea-leaves. Eleanore Atkins recalled that when Betty May lived in Skua Court, after she had finished her duties in the flat Betty May would insist on her staying, drinking tea and then reading her tea-leaves. Atkins said that she was able to "tell you the most fascinating things but seemed to be able to identify things from your past that did happen" (personal correspondence from Black to Author).

FORECASTS AND PREMONITIONS COMING TO FRUITION

Atkins recalled that Betty May told her from a tea-leaves reading that her mother had died when she was very young. This proved to be accurate as Atkins' mother died in 1945, when Atkins was just seventeen years old (ibid). Betty May also predicted that Atkins would eventually have grandchildren, "and there would be one boy who would be displaced and would have to grow up out of sight and away but he will come to you when you are older." This prediction came to pass and indeed a grandson was born and sent to live in South Africa as a child, years later he returned to England and lived with his grandmother (ibid). These examples show the accurate clairvoyant and mediumistic skills that Betty May possessed.

Her Kent pub friends recalled how clairvoyant and intriguing she was, one remarked "she could really see people, she could look at you and see an awful lot about you … people were frightened of her." A man had been teasing Betty May in the pub and she coldly said to him: "You're a horrible man and you're going to die a horrible death," and he did. She told another male customer chillingly: "Laugh as much as you like, because you're not long for here"..over a week later, he was dead (personal correspondence from Levy to Author).

Clearly, it was not wise for gentlemen to tease her or mock her psychic gifts. She was gentler with the female customers and staff in her local pubs, and was more sensitive about how she delivered the psychic information to them. Jane Dalley recalled that when she was a teenager and sat at the bar in the family-run pub in Rochester, she and Betty May used to sit together at the bar and talk about all kinds of different things. Dalley recalled how Betty May "classed herself as a white witch and, I have to say, predicted a lot correctly about my life ahead" (correspondence from Jane Dalley to Author). She predicted, for example, that the teenager would marry and live overseas; and this prediction came to pass. She also told the young girl's mother (just before her brother joined the army) that he would call for her over water, a long way away. Whilst in service, he drowned in Belize in Central America. So, eerily, Betty May's premonition once again had come to pass (ibid).

Returning again to the astrological aspect of Sun sextile Jupiter and her travelling overseas, some examples of her journeys include going to America, France and Italy and at the end of her autobiography, when she 35, she said that she was considering travelling again, possibly to Africa and also Spain (Betty May, 2014, p222).

Her visit to America in 1925 was one example of her escapades. This trip came about when she begged her friend, the author and influential newspaper editor, Bernard O' Donnell, to let her meet a celebrated American clairvoyant and telekinetic, 'Princess Waletka', who was visiting England and who had appeared in one of his newspapers. He agreed to Betty May's request and arranged for them all to meet for afternoon tea at the Waldorf Hotel (ibid, p195). They met and, apparently, the seeress invited Betty May to accompany her back to America to assist her on her next tour there. Betty May travelled there, as evidenced by the shipping documentation. It shows that on 6th August, the 'SS America' sailed from Southampton to America. It showed that Betty May Loveday was 30 years old and was a journalist (another fabrication!) who lived in Lewisham, London (www.nationalarchives.gov.uk). However, it didn't take long before Betty May became homesick and wanted to return back to London. Her host paid her fare home and gave her 100 pounds (Betty May, 2014, p201). The Author was unable to find any evidence of Betty May actually assisting Princess Waletka on her tour.

The desire for adventure and freedom is also connected with the Sun sextile Jupiter aspect. Overall, it is an optimistic and positive energy which would have helped Betty May look at unfortunate episodes in her life from a philosophical stance (as discussed previously). Her need for independence and wanting freedom as a child would certainly have been thwarted by any discipline and strictness in her younger years (as shown by Saturn in the fourth house in her natal chart).

Jupiter is associated with excess and so, when it comes to addressing Betty May's health, we know that her drink and drug intake were not taken in moderation. Of course, it doesn't follow that everyone with this aspect in their natal chart is going to either drink too much or take too many drugs. However, knowing what we do of Betty May's history and the symbolism of the twelfth house being associated with alcohol, drugs and addiction, it follows that it is another clue about her excessive nature.

FAITH, PROVIDENCE AND DIVINE INTERVENTION

One of Betty May's belief was in the journey of fate and she said: "I believe enormously in the overpowering influence of fate, which seems to haunt me equally in good or bad fortune" (Duckworth 2014, pp221,222). Jack Lindsay observed of her that "her driving force was a complete belief in her Fate – which in effect meant 'being herself', living in the dead-centre of herself" (Lindsay, 1962, p136). This shows just how much she believed in a guiding force and higher power that partly shaped her life and, given that she lived to 85, indicates the physical and spiritual strength of Betty May.

If she had knowledge of an astrological system called The Sabian Symbols (*see glossary*), she would have known that the symbol for her Sun in Virgo at 3 degrees is symbolised by "two guardian angels bringing protection" (Hill, 2004, p153), which is pertinent to her belief in a higher force watching over her during her life.

She was 35 when her book was published in 1929 and she declared: "I am still young; I have my looks and my energy. The future holds all sorts of things in store for me" (Duckworth, 2014, p221), showing her self-confidence and faith in herself and life itself. By the age of 35, she certainly had many adventures and experiences in life, perhaps more than some people have in a lifetime! Jupiter positioned in the twelfth house in her natal chart indicates that blessings and opportunities may have magically arrived at her feet. This in turn would have given her a certain optimism and philosophical stance about life, knowing that her well-developed intuition and psychic abilities would get her through (even in difficult circumstances), which indeed they must have, given that she lived to her mid-eighties! It seems that her faith was in life itself and fate gave her a form of 'protection' and that in itself was a kind of divine seal of approval.

David Garnett recalls Betty May in her younger years: "she was a terrific egoist and lived in a dream-world in which she was an important figure" (Garnett, 1955, p46). By this quote we can see the self-delusional and romanticising associations of Neptune (ruler of the twelfth house) at work. The results arising from the research of Betty May's life significantly show the astrology in action. There are many facets in astrology, so the potential of symbolism is vast, this we can certainly see through the aspects and planets in the twelfth house of Betty May's natal chart. The energy is particularly potent in that area, since not only is Neptune present in the twelfth house, its ruler in the natural zodiac, but Jupiter is also present and this planet used to be the ruler of the twelfth house in traditional astrology. The famous traditional (*see glossary*) astrologer, William Lilly, identified that witches were associated with the twelfth house and this may be pertinent as to why today in modern astrology, mysticism is associated with the twelfth house, as is magic and spirituality.

In her later years, Betty May used to visit the local Spiritualist church (personal correspondence from Ben Levy to Author). It is possible that this may have been in New Road, Rochester in Kent. Whether she had always been a follower of the Spiritualist religion is unknown, but seemingly she found comfort from it when she was a pensioner and, after all, she like so many others had lost many friends (and family members) as a result of the two

World Wars. It is unclear whether she demonstrated clairvoyance at the church as an invited medium, or whether she attended as part of the congregation. The Author has been unable to find any documents or records which pertain to her serving as a platform medium in the New Road Spiritualist church, although one could easily see her performing in such a role, given how she adored an audience, was clairvoyant and mediumistic.

Associations of the twelfth house allude to other themes such as dissolution, escapism and intangibility, as well as institutions (such as hospitals and prisons). We know already that Betty May had been in the workhouse and its infirmary when she was a teenager. However, when she was 23, she was in a French prison for a short period of time along with her partner, Edgell Rickword, and two of their friends. The reason for this was that they had insufficient funds to pay for their hotel bill, where they had stayed for a few days in Dieppe (*Daily Express*, 06/02/1918).

DECEPTION, ELUSIVENESS AND RITUAL

Other areas which are associated with Neptune, the ruler of the twelfth house, includes that which is hidden, for example; clandestine activities and secrets, mystery, deception and illusion, as well as elusiveness and scandal. Betty May was known to magically do 'disappearing acts' where she would not tell others where she was going or where she had been for reasons known only to herself. Garnett recalls how "she would spend an evening with me and then disappear for a week or two, only to greet me with delight when we met again" (Garnett, 1955, p46). Secrecy and unseen business are also associated with Neptune in the twelfth house and can include areas such as different aliases and stage-names. This is true of 'Betty May' in that she never returned to using her given name of Bessie Golding and she used other assumed names, for example; Betty Marlow Golding (marriage certificate to Atkinson in 1914) and Betty May

Bailey (1939 Register). She told W.B. Seabrook in a newspaper interview: "I was born Marlow Golding in the slums of this city" (*Evansville Courier*, Seabrook, 1928, p2), the name being yet another fabrication. Atkins, who (as previously mentioned) was her home-help in the early 1970's, said of her: "She seemed like she always wanted to tell you a secret but you thought she just made it up if she even did tell you." This was when Betty May was in her mid-70's and whether the secret was true or untrue ... who knows?

A name that she used for magical purposes at Crowley's Abbey of Thelema in Cefalù was 'Sister Sibylline' – the name meaning 'prophetic'. Whilst staying at the Abbey, she was required to wear loose robes of bright blue with scarlet linings, hood and golden girdle (Lindsay, 1962, p134). At the Abbey, sex-magic was "carried out to the accompaniment of hymns, prayers and symbolic performances" (Lindsay, 1962, p133). Betty May recalled that "every Friday night there was a special invocation to Pan" (Betty May, 2014, p173). When the Loveday's first arrived at the Abbey of Thelema, they became aware of the words painted on the main door of the low white house, which read: "Do What Thou Wilt Shall Be The Whole Of The Law." This was the password of those within the Abbey and their invariable greeting (100thmonkeypress.com). The 'temple' "was a large square room out of which the other five rooms opened. We noticed at once a Pompeian censer of bronze and a six-sided altar standing in the centre of a magick circle that was painted on the tile floor" (ibid).

Symbolism is plentiful in astrology. We can see further associations of Neptune in the twelfth house which are relevant to Betty May, which include the following: dance, music and fashion, glamour and photography, which is borne out by her time as an artist's and photographer's model, as well as her love of dance and singing. She said in her autobiography that: "Dancing is my natural mode of expression. When I am one. My mind, my spirit, my me, and my body is all and each of them" (Betty

May, 2014, p70). As a child, when she was staying on the barge with her great aunt and great uncle, she quickly found a way of gaining attention and appreciation by dancing and singing for the sailors whenever they passed by on a ship, they enjoyed her performance and threw pennies to her. She wrote that during her childhood she "had never danced before, but it came quite easily to me" (Betty May, 1929, p27).

As far as clandestine activities are concerned, she was involved in secret relationships, which seems to have suited her quite well, as it didn't cramp her style by being a mistress – so retaining her independence and this is indicated by Uranus in the fifth house of her natal chart. One example of this is with Australian-born author and publisher, Jack Lindsay, who lived in England. He had a partner, Elza, who lived in Essex (where he stayed when he was not in London) and before starting a physical relationship with Betty May, he told her all about the other woman – but Elza was never told about Betty May. Lindsay said of Betty May that "she made no bones about going with others while I was in the country" (Lindsay, 1962, p135).

ADDICTION AND DEPENDENCY

There are also other Neptune correspondences which include alcohol and drugs. She became an addict and claimed in her autobiography that her second husband divorced her because of her dependency on drugs (http://www.elisarolle.com/). The divorce papers state otherwise, showing that George Dibbs King Waldron divorced her on the grounds of 'frequently committed adultery' with Leonard E. Van Leer of London (National Archives/ref:J77/14900/6030). However, she did apparently cure herself from her dependence on drugs. Aleister Crowley commented on how impressed he was that, after years of drug addiction where Betty May had been using a quarter of an ounce or more daily of cocaine, Betty May managed to cure herself. He said that she showed "superb courage in curing herself" (Symonds & Grant, 1979, p904). This she did by at first switching over to injections of morphia and then from that on to alcohol (ibid) – she had swapped one addiction for another. She said in her autobiography that "the craving for drugs was an awful bondage" (Betty May, 2014, p106) … "I remember the excitements I got out of it all and must admit that I enjoyed them" (ibid).

Further on she reflected: "I love feeling free more than anything else in the world and when one is taking drugs seriously, one never does feel free. Often I lost my voice entirely" (ibid). Other side-effects from taking cocaine include involuntary grinding of the teeth and after the euphoria of taking the drug comes depression (Kohn, 1992, p124). She spoke candidly to Seabrook about the effects of drug dependency and said that "I got so low and depressed that I was thinking of suicide" (*Evansville Courier*, Seabrook, 1928, p37). She also said to Seabrook that she "was one of the biggest dope fiends in London … as Scotland Yard knows full well" (ibid), indicating that she was criminally known to the police and also known to the underworld.

Betty May had a near-death-experience after a friend of hers gave her the drug Amyl Nitrate Five-M to try, which had a transforming effect on her life. This was after she had returned from Sicily after the death of Raoul Loveday. Then she took to drugs even more seriously than before, she confided to Seabrook that she believed "there was some kind of curse on her and that black despair followed whatever she attempted to do … and that she was practically in the gutter" (ibid).

She confided in Seabrook after she took the drug that "my whole life came panoramically past me, like a drowning person's. I saw that my life had been futile, stupid and wrong" (ibid). It was after this that she realised she had been given a second chance in life and was adamant to wean herself off drugs. There are parts of her birth chart (as discussed earlier) which show that she had qualities of determination and purpose which would help her to achieve her goals if she put her mind to it. She further added that after that episode, she told herself "I'll pull myself together NOW. And I have" (ibid), which shows her strength of mind and willpower. However, as time went on, she had swapped one dependency for another, drugs being replaced by alcohol.

Qualities of Neptune also include loss, suffering, wounding and vulnerability. Certainly, as previously discussed, she experienced (like many others) the loss of friends during the two World Wars. For example, there was her friend Laura Grey the actress and suffragette who died. She took a drugs overdose and was found dead in 1914. Two of Betty May's husbands died too young – her first husband was killed during the First World War and her third husband died in Cefalù from enteritis. As we already know, at an early age there were breaks from her parents in terms of her upbringing and she never seemed to be able to settle anywhere, either as a child or an adult – not only through poverty but also restlessness and a dream of escape for a better existence, yearning constantly for adventure and grander pastures.

LUNAR ASPECTS, FANTASY AND LOSS

Looking at the Moon aspects and planets in the twelfth house, we can see at a deeper level how these may have manifested and played out in Betty May's life. There are three aspects created with the Moon: Moon conjunct Neptune, Moon conjunct Pluto and Moon square the MC. Interestingly, her MC (the mid-heaven, *see glossary*) sign is Pisces – the MC is associated with career and profession and Pisces, as already discussed, is ruled by Neptune in the natural zodiac. It is unsurprising therefore that she worked in the areas of dancing, modelling and singing – areas where she could create illusions and moods using her imagination.

The Moon (as previously mentioned) is square the MC and shows that she dreamt of the aforementioned areas, but they may have been short-lived, as both the Gemini Moon and Pisces MC belong to the fluctuating and variable mutable mode. This shows that commitments and reliability could have been challenging for her. Betty May's moodiness and her temperamental nature may at times have got in the way of her career, as well as any potential work opportunities, especially during the period in her life when she was an addict. Her reputation went before her and seemed to both help and hinder her at the same time.

Moon conjunct Neptune shows that she had a fertile imagination, could be enchanting and spellbinding and, at times, could be virtually oblivious that she was fantasising. The placement of Neptune in Gemini would have added to an ability of creative storytelling, it also indicates that she may have had a clever though complicated mind. This would have been helpful to her in her work as a photographer's model, as well as when she was singing. In these areas she could have channelled her creativity and imagination.

A small, although derogatory, example of this can be seen by a conclusion of Atkins who said: "I think she liked you to believe that she could do anything and had been someone" (personal correspondence from Ian Black to Author). This is concurred somewhat when Seabrook said at the end of his interview with Betty May that "she looked at me to see whether I believed her," and he told the readers of the newspaper that he did. However, six years later, she confessed in court (as discussed earlier) that parts of her autobiography were fictional, and this included areas of her life that she had discussed with Seabrook. This shows that she was able to weave fantasies about her past, which would have enabled her to escape from reality, maintain her privacy and remain secretive about her life. Her deceit when being interviewed by Seabrook also illustrates Kaldera's interpretation about the manipulative 'Magician's Moon', which was discussed earlier.

The aspect between the Moon and Neptune also holds symbolism for a 'lost mother' and 'mother being a victim' through the Moon representing the care-taking figure and Neptune and in the twelfth house symbolising loss and oppression. This is especially significant to Betty May as genealogical records about her mother Ellen stop at approximately 1906, with not even a death certificate to be found. Betty May slights both parents in a newspaper article by W.B. Seabrook, claiming that "my parents were nothing to brag about; they were shiftless and now and then they drank" (*Evansville Courier,* Seabrook, 1928, p2).

The Moon conjunct Neptune can indicate that if the mother-figure was lost, other people cared for her. This is borne out by her paternal grandparents caring for her as a child and also the workhouse warden when she was a teenager. History shows us that she expected to be cared for by other people in adulthood too, especially in a financial away, as illustrated by her relationship with David Garnett which shows she had a lack of self-responsibility and an inability to manage her finances and resources.

Other interpretations of the Moon conjunct Neptune and the Cancer ascendant also show that she was open to the influence of motherly figures. One example of this is borne out through her affection for Jacob Epstein's wife, Peggy. When Betty May first met Mr and Mrs Epstein, she said of Peggy that "she seems to me to be an absolute perfect wife for a great sculptor" (Betty May, 1929, p114). She continued: "I got to know what a magnificent woman Mrs Epstein is, and how she understands looking after an artist ... she knows just when to have a meal ready ... what a pity every man of genius cannot have such a wife" (ibid, p115). This also shows the Capricorn descendant at work, in that Betty May was attracted to traditions such as marriage, but what attracted her and what satisfied her were two *very* different things. Author and astrologer, Jeanne Avery, observed that people with Cancer on the ascendant can feel a distinct lack of mothering and tender loving care from childhood, as well as feeling abandoned early in their life (Avery, 1982, p126). This is something that Betty May could have felt from her formative years when, as we know, she was the responsibility of different care-givers over a short period of time. Avery's observation concurs with some of the astrological data in Betty May's chart, such as Saturn in the fourth house and the Moon in the twelfth house.

Neptune is square the MC and this suggests that when she was growing up there was some kind of disadvantage; poverty being one example, also those areas of experience may have included confusion and guilt which are associated with this planet. Notoriety and scandal are also correspondences of Neptune. Therefore, it is unsurprising perhaps that Betty May appeared in both local and national newspapers during her lifetime concerning various subjects which brought her into the spotlight and which ensured a financial reward for her story and no doubt would have caused gossip and speculation in her family (as well as other readers of the newspapers!). Another possibility of Neptune square the MC is that one of her parents was absent or a parent may have weakened the family due to alcohol, drugs or sickness (associations of Neptune). We know already that when Betty May was approximately fourteen years old, her mother had disappeared from the Golding family – around 1906. By that time, and as already discussed, Betty May had already been cared for by a variety of family members.

SURVIVAL, PERCEPTION AND UNPREDICTABILITY

The Moon conjunct Pluto in the twelfth house also holds associations of concealment, mystery and silence. Crisis, emotional turmoil and trauma may have been experienced when she was a child, which she may have buried in her unconscious as a coping mechanism and as a way of helping her to survive. By keeping those experiences concealed, it may have harmed her in the long run, affecting her well-being and leading to patterns of detrimental behaviour to herself and ultimately to other people.

BETTY MAY (1894–1980)

Pluto in the twelfth house not only suggests privacy and secrecy but is also a sign of a great inner strength and power, the latter can be seen by way of her being able to probe beneath the surface and feel what is going on behind the scenes. This is borne out by the example of her being able to provide psychic readings for people by reading their palms. The lesson for her in this would be how to maintain that confidentiality and not misuse her power. The Moon in the twelfth house also added to her intuitive nature and this natural gift would have helped her to keep one step ahead of the game, which ultimately would have added to her fight for survival and strengthened her instinctive 'street-nouse'.

Uranus is quincunx Pluto and indicates that Betty May was passionate, perhaps even obsessed with being different and rebellious. Uranus is associated with shock and so it could be argued that she had a compulsion almost to alarm others, perhaps manipulating them by playing on their anxieties. This compulsion may have led her to becoming anxious and tense, if she was driven to be outrageous and shocking; such is the rebellious and unpredictable nature of Uranus. One example of this can be seen by the following illustration: Jacob Epstein recalled in his autobiography (in approximately 1914) how artist, Jacob Kramer, was similar to Betty May and described him as a true Bohemian. Epstein was awoken in the early hours of the morning by Kramer who pleaded with him to go to court to speak for Betty May. "She had thrown a glass at an enemy of Epstein's in a café dispute. Upon attending, he found Betty May there with all her friends in the court" (Epstein, 2014, Kindle). "She was excited and happy at the situation and smiled to everyone" (ibid). In answering the magistrate, he said of Betty May that she was, to his knowledge, "most gentle but temperamental and must have been provoked" (ibid). The magistrate repeated: "Gentle but temperamental. Three Pounds." After hearing the magistrate's ruling, "the happy band of Bohemians went to the Café Royal for drinks" (ibid).

The aforementioned sum of money was equivalent in today's money to approximately 112 pounds, which was considerable then – did she expect Epstein or Kramer to pay her fine for her? Given that she was in Epstein's words "excited" and "happy" at the situation, perhaps she did expect to be bailed out by either of the two men. Her rebellious and unpredictable (not to mention irresponsible) behaviour both at the court and in the café shows she had no regret or remorse for her action – showing the outrageous and shocking energy of Uranus and how she enjoyed the buzz and excitement of the situation. By throwing the glass at Epstein's friend, it also shows the aggressive and impulsive Sun trine Mars aspect in action, which was discussed earlier on.

ART, MODELLING AND AN ALTERNATIVE STYLE

Previously, the area of glamour was discussed as an association of the twelfth house. There is further indication in Betty May's natal chart about this theme, by the position of Venus being in the second house and, in the natural zodiac (*see glossary*), Venus is at home in that position. It shows how she valued clothes, finery and style, as well as beauty-products and also art. In the mid-late 1960's, her pub friends recalled how she regularly powdered her face to make it look paler. One of the friends recalled how Betty May "had lovely skin" and they also remembered that "she wore old clothes but they were expensive clothes" (personal correspondence from Ben Levy to Author) – clearly the quality of the clothes had stood the test of time. Betty May remained distinctive and stylish throughout her life and those same aforementioned friends recalled how she wore a red beret and red lipstick and also that she adorned a blue mackintosh with a belt and little black pumps (ibid). Interestingly, author and astrologer, Jeanne Avery, observed that for people with Cancer on their ascendant "colour is especially essential for the sensitive nature" (Avery, 1982, p134).

BETTY MAY (1894–1980)

The second house also indicates our possessions and also how one earns a living. The placement of Venus in the second house is pertinent to Betty May, as one of her assets was her personal attractiveness and style and, as we know, she earned her living by using her body for modelling and sitting for artists and photographers. There are several photographs of her in the public domain where she can be seen modelling hats and other unusual items of clothing from the day. Venus is square Uranus in her natal chart and this shows that she dressed in a unique way and liked to stand out from the crowd or go for an avant-garde look. This is borne out when she said in her autobiography that once she was able to afford to buy new clothing, "dressed then in the brilliant colours that are my right and heritage, my personality burst suddenly forth in its full peculiarity" (Betty May, 2014, p40).

There is another example of her Bohemian style – her hairstyle. When she was a young child and teenager, she had long hair and sometimes wore it in plaits (ibid, p43) which was the norm for somebody of her age and class then. However, when she decided to have her hair cut and styled into the then controversial 'bob-style' we do not know. Certainly, in the 1920's, the style was becoming more fashionable, there were different types of 'bob' hairstyles too. During that period, that particular haircut was considered controversial, as it was seen by mainstream society that women were trying to act like men and rebelling against the beauty standards of the time (https://fashionista.com/). It became associated with the 'shocking' behaviour of young women

By kind permission of The Warburg Institute, SAS, University of London.

who drank alcohol, wore make-up and bared their knees – it was a permanent signifier of a woman's rebellious nature (ibid). This behaviour was certainly true of Betty May and she virtually retained the same hairstyle until her dying days – short, almost curly but crinkly hair that had turned white (personal correspondence from Levy to Author). The bob hairstyle became associated with the Flappers in the 1920's, as well as many American actresses of that period. Through her choice of adorning an unusual dress style and haircut, we can see the Venus square Uranus aspect in action. It demonstrates how Betty May dressed for herself and not to please others, she did not wish to conform to standard beauty and dress-code of the day.

Uranus is positioned in Scorpio and shows how she was indomitable, strong-willed and determined to make a distinctive and unforgettable mark on the society in which she was born and lived. Dolores, the infamous artists' model (as noted earlier), said: "In this revolt against the claims of convention, I was ably seconded by Betty May, a glittering and sinister figure in London night-life" (*Pittsburgh Sun. Telegraph*, Dolores, 1930, page number unknown).

Venus is in Leo in her natal chart and indicates that she valued comfort and luxury and had an artistic and creative leaning. Through the medium of art and music, one can give and receive pleasure. Betty May was able to express love and other themes through her dancing and singing, and through her modelling work was able to offer pleasure to her audiences. The position of Venus in Leo is perfect for acting, which is often needed in art and photography by way of striking a pose to create an image. Presumably, Betty May must have valued Basil as an artist too, and appreciated the results of his photographic work; given that she worked for him frequently. She continued to enjoy dancing and music through to her later life and pub-friends remembered how she used to love the music of David Bowie and Elton John and how she would fling her arms in the air and twirl as she was dancing (personal correspondence from Ben Levy to Author).

The Moon quincunx Uranus in her natal chart shows that she would have been at home in a creative industry where her originality could come to the fore, but in an environment which was not imbued with co-workers and time-critical duties. Her reputation was built on her erratic and moody behaviour, as well as an unwillingness to follow orders and prescribe to the established way of doing things. It appears that she and Basil had a mutual respect and understanding for each other.

In *The Confessions of Aleister Crowley*, when he wrote about Betty May, one of the things he claimed was that "one day she brought out a fat package of photographs herself in the nude" (edited by Symonds & Grant, 1979, p912). Possibly, these were photographs that Basil had taken of her or maybe they were from another photographer. Like so many models, her career was short-lived. As far as we know, she didn't work in any other regular artistic capacity after working with Basil, who died in 1956. Being self-employed must have brought periods of financial unpredictability, which in turn may have put a strain on her nervous system, making her feel edgy and even causing extremes of emotions – such are some of the associations connected with the Moon quincunx Uranus aspect. She relied on others to financially support her, for example; David Garnett, and 'Billy' Barfoot.

DRAMA, GRANDIOSE AND SPECTACLE

Mercury is also in Leo and in the third house in her natal chart. This shows that she could express herself in a dramatic way, which would be helpful for performance work, as well as her arguments! David Garnett recalled how, in a row with her, she "struck an attitude of outraged virtue and began a melodramatic scene ... she dug her nails into my arm, but suddenly the pretence of anger turned to love and I was almost suffocated with fierce kisses" (Garnett, 1955, p44), which shows how she was spontaneous and unpredictable. When she was in her seventies, customers from her local pub recall fondly her "dramatic way" and that when she laughed she would "throw her head back in a theatrical way." Even when she smoked a cigarette, she would hold it in such an elegant way so that it was left dangling limp in her hand but in a graceful way. She continued to smoke, right through her life (personal correspondence from Levy to Author).

The aforementioned planetary position also shows an extrovert and confident speaking style which at times can also be boastful and dogmatic. One example of her high-and-mighty and haughty nature can be seen by the following: she used to regularly snap her fingers at everybody (Duckworth, 2014, p106) when she wanted something (which is arrogant and self-aggrandising to say the least). She also used to beckon people with her index finger and say: "I need to tell you something," usually this was followed by confidential and precognitive information by way of her psychic readings (personal correspondence from Levy to Author). This way of communicating shows the Mercury in Leo energy in her conceited and high-and-mighty manner.

Her pub acquaintances recall how she spoke beautifully in a natural way (ibid). However, Eleanore Atkins recalled that Betty May "had the most frightfully posh voice but would occasionally slip up and talk like someone from the gutter and use gutter language … then recompose herself … she was very endearing" (personal correspondence from Ian Black to Author). Clearly, Betty May imitated an accent and language that she was familiar with and could mimic when she chose, which shows another form of her acting ability. The positions of Mercury in Leo and the aforementioned planets in the twelfth house of her natal chart, indicate her ability to disguise, mimic and create illusions.

Conversely, there is also a warmth with Mercury and Venus in Leo, whereby Betty May could be generous and warm in spirit. A friend of hers from The Man of Kent pub described her as "having a good heart but was lonely" (personal correspondence from Dalley to Author). This was backed up by Betty May's letters to her friend, Garnett, and an example given is when she wrote to him in November, 1972, and said that she felt lonely (Northwestern University Special Collections Letters).

TEMPORARILY TAKING CARE OF OTHERS

The position of Jupiter in Cancer in her natal chart shows that she could also be open-hearted when playing hostess and enjoyed the pleasures of the home. This position also shows the potential for the enjoyment of taking care of people and of home-life. There are some illustrations of how this manifested in her later life. However, because Cancer is ruled by the Moon and her Moon sign is positioned in Gemini, it reveals that being a hostess as well as a constant carer would not have been satisfying to her on a long-term basis. This is because the Moon's energy is fluctuating, whilst the energy of Gemini is flighty and changeable.

Nonetheless, in the 1930's, she helped the management of the Fitzroy Tavern with their 'Pennies from Heaven' fund. This was set up with donations from the customers and patrons to mainly help the many local disadvantaged and impoverished children (previously it had helped senior citizens). The fund enabled many children to have days out so they could visit places that ordinarily they may not have had the opportunity to, for example; Southend, so they could experience a day at the seaside. Betty May was called upon as a helper with the groups of children along with many other famous people of the time who used to frequent the Fitzroy Tavern whilst they went out on their adventures. This may have suited Betty May as she could be enthusiastic and inspiring in a group; this is borne out by the position of Mars in the eleventh house (as discussed previously) and because it was not a daily event, it would have appealed to her agitated and restless nature.

When she was staying at the Abbey in Cefalù with Crowley and her husband, she was given the responsibility of carrying out the cooking, shopping and other household duties as well as looking after the three little children who were also staying there (Betty May, 2014, p162). Betty May said that the coffee and wine that she drunk there was some of the best that she had ever had (ibid, pp163,166). The main foodstuffs that they ate there were Sicilian bread, cream-cheese made from goat's milk and meat (ibid, p162).

Astonishingly, her talents for her cooking abilities reached a national newspaper in 1929 when the *Daily Mirror* reported that Betty May was proud of her cooking and that for two years she was cook to Jacob Epstein and his family (*Daily Mirror*, 1929, page and journalist unknown). Her talents for cooking were noted by poet, Malcolm Lowry, and his wife, Jan Gabriel, when they met her several times in the autumn of 1933 when she was staying at South Hill Park Gardens in Hampstead with Hugh Sykes Davies. A diary entry by Gabriel reveals her thoughts about Betty May: "She is fascinating, warm, friendly and very attractive, as well as a wizard cook" (guttedarcades.blogspot.com). She then goes on to say that she and Lowry were invited back the following evening to dine with Betty May and her former lover, Edgell Rickword. Afterwards, they all went out for drinks at her regular haunts. Having started at the Fitzroy Tavern, they went on to the Marquis of Granby and The Plough and then finished the evening by going on to Smokey Joe's, which was a non-alcoholic-speakeasy-cum-lesbian pub (ibid).

This shows the generous and warm-hearted nature of Betty May and that, when she was in the right mood and had congenial company, she could be engaging and sociable. It also shows that she enjoyed a sense of the risqué, too. Another review of this club, however, described it as "a basement members' club or 'bottle club', a very bad place indeed" (Avery & Graham, 2018, p233). If the club was notorious and not twee, as the original description suggests, then Betty May would have been at home there and unperturbed by what others thought of her. Entertainment for her needed to be original and stimulating and this is shown by Uranus in the fifth house.

Other themes that are associated with the fifth house are creativity, love affairs, children and self-expression. We have already seen how she was creative and expressive through her modelling and singing and that she had a unique sense of design and stylishness in her appearance.

ACCIDENTS, CHILDHOOD AND FREEDOM

When it comes to children, Uranus in the fifth house suggests that having children would have hampered Betty May's freedom, particularly in her modelling years. This is because Uranus is associated with being unrestricted and unconventional and also with free will and independence. Being a parent may have been dull and irritating to her. Uranus in the fifth house also provides some insight as to the qualities of herself as a child. The energy of both Uranus and the fifth house are associated with the fixed mode (see glossary) and this indicates that she was a determined and wilful child and may not have responded well to authority and discipline. This is because Uranus is associated with freedom and rebellion.

In her autobiography and reflecting upon her stay with her relatives on the barge, she said: "I have never wanted to be different from what I am ... and fled from any influence that seemed likely to alter my personality" (Betty May, 2014, p26). This seems somewhat contradictory in the sense that her addictions were one obvious influence that inevitably altered her personality and another example includes the change of her accent, depending on her audience.

Other themes connected with Uranus include accidents and shocks. This is interesting with regards to information claimed about Betty May by Aleister Crowley. He wrote that: "In her childhood, an accident had damaged her brain permanently so that its functions were discontinuous" (Symonds & Grant, 1979, p904). Whether this information was volunteered to him by Betty May is unknown, if she did, it may or may not have been true (as we know already) – she was prone to a fertile imagination. If she didn't say this then it may have been Crowley being malicious about her, and not for the first time either. He unkindly called her a "half-crazed whore, who had been twice married and once divorced" (Kaczynski, 2010, p383). Perhaps he recognised some of himself in her which led him to be so malevolent about her; a woman equally as liberated as he was, and his projection reflecting the similarities in himself.

Love affairs and romance are also associated with the fifth house as noted earlier and Uranus placed in this position suggests the following: her love affairs may have been erratic, that she may have been drawn to unconventional types (like the Bohemians) who shared her love of the unusual and also enjoyed living on the edge. She may have had an unpredictable love-life where sudden break ups were part of the picture, as were sudden infatuations with people. Uranus in Scorpio also shows that she was deeply intuitive and strong-willed as well as charismatic and determined.

THE BUSINESS OF RELATIONSHIPS AND SEX

Venus is square Uranus in her natal chart (as previously discussed) and this aspect indicates that she was impetuous and reckless in her relationships (as we have indeed seen from earlier examples) and that she also sought the thrill of the forbidden (such as partners already in committed relationships). She would have sought excitement, freedom and independence in her partnerships, free love and open relationships would have appealed to her. This is borne out in one example, in the case of her relationship with Jack Lindsay. She was his mistress and he told her that he also had a partner (Elza) in Essex; this suited Betty May as it gave her freedom to sleep with whom she wanted whilst Lindsay was living with his wife. When they met up in London after he had spent some time with his wife, she cheerfully told him how she spent the night in a shop which sold beds. The key-holder pulled down the shop blinds and selected a bed for them to partake in the act (Lindsay, 1962, p135).

It is believed that Betty May was a sex-worker and started at a young age. For example, Jack Lindsay wrote that when she was very young "she drifted into a pick-up life" (ibid, p132). It is also believed that she was engaged in prostitution from when she was approximately fourteen years old (personal correspondence from Levy to Author). Although we have no evidence of this, it certainly would have been a swift way of getting money to support her addictions and basic needs when she was a younger woman. However, she was in formal employment when she was seventeen, as a servant in a farmhouse in Surrey. When she returned from there, she admitted herself into the workhouse (as noted earlier).

Venus square Uranus in Scorpio also hints at 'money for sex' and this is because Venus is associated with relationships and money, Scorpio with sex and Uranus with the disconnected and impersonal. Mars is also square Venus which shows that her love-life may have been troubled with arguments and unhappiness but also cushioned with passion and tension. This we saw in an earlier example, when David Garnett described how she turned from a mood of pretend anger into intense passion. She seemed to invest her energy into thriving on romantic and sexual involvements, where a stormy relationship would be inevitable. Venus in Leo would have been at home with such dramas and performances in relationships, for the excitement and thrill of it all.

Uranus is also associated with experimentation, so with the Venus square aspect it is perhaps unsurprising that Betty May enjoyed a sex-life with men and women. In her later years, she confided in a female 'pub-friend' that she was bisexual (ibid) and that she "had done everything sexual in her life" (ibid), perhaps that 'everything' included prostitution. She remained open-minded in her later years and her pub-friends knew about a friendship that she had at that time with an elderly lesbian who was one of the few people who were allowed to visit Betty May at her flat.

RESTRICTIONS AND INFRINGEMENT OF SELF-EXPRESSION

Betty May never forgot her experiences of marriage or other relationships and counselled another male 'pub-friend' advising that, "If you want to keep your wife, don't tie her down. If you tie women down they'll leave" (personal correspondence from Ben Levy to Author). When she first met her fourth husband in a newspaper office, she quickly realised what kind of man Noel Mostyn Sedgwick was. She described him as "assertive" and "opinionated", for his first remark to her was: "I wish you'd take some of the rouge off your lips. I think it looks horrible. And I detest polished nails" (Betty May, 2014, p202). His remarks did not deter her and they started to dine and lunch together each day. However, his chauvinistic opinions were engrained in him, as he retorted to Betty May that a woman must be "well turned out" (ibid, p203). His comments, however, did not discourage her and they married shortly afterwards. She must have resented his bigoted opinions and inevitably she got bored with him, as well as living in the countryside which lacked the variety and fast-paced life that London offered her, it was inevitable that the marriage would not survive. In 1930, Sedgwick petitioned for divorce on the grounds of her adultery, the co-respondent being

Edgell Rickwood (National Archives, Divorce Court/File 7182). The certificate of their Decree Nisi Absolute (divorce) shows that Sedgwick petitioned for divorce on 9th March, 1931, and it was made final and absolute on 16th September, 1931 (Court of High Justice, Family Division/No.74 of 1931). There were no co-respondents named on the certificate, so from that document it remains unknown whether Sedgwick petitioned for divorce on the grounds of adultery, desertion, separation or unreasonable behaviour.

In her natal chart, Saturn is in Libra (and exalted, *see glossary*) and this suggests that she would have found relationships limiting and testing. Mercury is sextile Saturn in her natal chart and suggests that she had a logical and pragmatic attitude towards partnerships; she could be canny and shrewd in her thinking regarding both business and personal relationships. Betty May was married four times and this was approximately every two years, therefore she must have been regularly thinking about her security and finding a husband/partner to provide and pay for a comfortable home for her.

Given that Saturn is also associated with fear and Libra with relationships, this suggests that she may have had a fear about being alone and not in a long-term partnership. If she was in a long-term partnership, it would have had to have been on her terms, where her partner understood that she needed independence, excitement and freedom. Astrologers, Joy Michaud and Karen Hilverson, observed that for people who have Saturn in Libra in their natal charts they "often go through very disappointing and painful episodes in connection to relationships ... before realizing that all they see within others is but a reflection of their own psyche" (Michaud & Hilverson, 1993, p24), which is pertinent to what we know of Betty May and her personal partnerships.

Perhaps one of her most testing partnerships was with Hubert William 'Billy' Barfoot (Bailey). This is because letters that

Betty May sent to David Garnett in 1961 and 1962 (McCormick Special Collections Archives, Northwestern University) claim that 'Billy' had been treating her badly. According to her, he had been depriving her of any money and he was also in serious debt. Not only that but he was also having an affair with a much younger woman, who was a local publican and who had a two year old daughter and Barfoot would not leave the pub until after closing time. By 1962, Barfoot's health had deteriorated. He had problems with his chest and numerous unspecified other health problems, he was bedridden and Betty May had fallen into the role of his full-time carer, which must have been exceptionally hard and testing for her, given she was then in her late sixties, and if what she claims about Billy and his behaviour was true.

Aware of being a man's property and losing her individuality and her own voice was an area that she clearly had been scarred by through her four marriages. She advised a close female teenage 'pub-friend' of hers in the 1970's that after she has married, "Never ever let a man own you just because he has given you his name, and you don't have to take his name, you are never a man's property" (correspondence from Jane Dalley to Author).

This is ironic, especially the latter advice about not being a man's property, given that Betty May kept the surname Sedgwick, even after her divorce and it was that name that was on her death certificate, she must have had her personal reasons for keeping her married name of Sedgwick. Her advice to Dalley though is certainly in keeping with the independent side to her Virgo nature.

SPIRITUAL ADVICE

In astrology, there is an area which indicates karmic points in one's life, which are called the Moon's nodes (*see glossary*); they are the north node and south node. They are believed to give you guidance on how to live your life in order to advance on your spiritual path. The north node indicates qualities that one should develop, whilst the south node indicates qualities that one should inhibit. Betty May's natal chart shows that the north node is in Aries and the south node is in Libra.

The north node in Aries suggests that in her lifetime (1894–1980) she needed to be more assertive and have self-confidence and be less concerned about compromising with other people. It could be said from what we know about her that she was indeed confident. However, in terms of cooperation that is more difficult to see, at least from what we know about her. The north node is in the tenth house and indicates that in her professional work she would have chosen to undertake a competitive field in order to gain her reputation. This is borne out in the arena of modelling where Betty May gained her reputation as an artist's model. The node's position also indicates that by asserting herself in a professional world and by being independent and unafraid to take control in her work, that it would help her to reconcile any residue karma from a previous incarnation. Both Aries and the tenth house belong to the cardinal mode (*see glossary*), which shows that Betty May was capable of initiating and leading in professional situations if she so wished.

TRANSITS AND THE COMPLETED CYCLE OF LIFE

Betty May died in 1980 and existing letters (Northwestern University, Special Collections/Letters) written by her to her lifelong saviour, David Garnett, reveal when she started to feel frail, unwell and lonely in her later life. Billy Barfoot went into hospital in 1962 and died there in 1963. Having lived with him for 24 years, she wrote to Garnett after his death and said in a postscript that she felt desolate. Previously, in 1961, Betty May wrote to Garnett and claimed that her common-law husband had been "behaving dreadfully" – he had affairs whilst living with her and had denied her any money for her old-age pension. Interestingly, the probate documents for Barfoot's parents show that he was not left anything by them in their will and we can only speculate as to why, especially given that he was an only child.

In 1963, after Barfoot's death, she wrote to Garnett and told him that she wasn't sleeping very well and then in the March of the same year wrote and told him that she had been diagnosed with angina and prescribed pills to take for the condition. The medication may have helped her emotional and mental health too; she told him that she didn't feel quite as lonely as she had previously. In 1964, she told Garnett that she had been informed by the local authority housing committee that she had been awarded a flat. This was in Skua Court, her final home, and was a warden-controlled block for the elderly. Betty May was concerned that the flat was "way out in the wilds," one can sense her trepidation of feeling isolated there. However, before she could collect her keys and rent book for her new flat, she had to pay a debt of four pounds, as well as paying one weeks rent in advance. She asked Garnett for a loan of fifteen pounds, in order to pay off her "fearful debts" and to buy new items for her flat. In virtually all the letters held by the Northwestern University, she asks Garnett if he will loan her money. This dependency on Garnett's money started when she was a teenager, and he was an enabler in that he allowed the practice to carry on, in that he would give her cash (later on cheques) even when she was married or in other partnerships. One cannot help wonder how she always seemed to be in debt (at least when she wrote to Garnett she claimed to be) and unable to manage her finances and resources.

Clearly, her attitude towards money was an unusual one and seemingly she expected to be supported financially by others, as far as we know she did not make any attempt to earn her own money after her short-lived career as an artist's model. This may account for why, as a young woman, she changed her name so often and deliberately put false information on documents if she owed money to different people. Her outlook about money may also have been shaped by her fatalistic and optimistic view about life, in thinking that something would turn up and it will be alright ... and it usually did! This is a very different approach to matters involving money whereby, generally speaking, Virgos are usually concerned and organised about money matters. The Venus square Uranus aspect in her chart also suggests money coming unexpectedly when there seems to be problems arising around money issues. Her dependency on alcohol may also have contributed to her financial position throughout most of her life, prioritising her addiction over other essential areas of life; one example being her rent. After she died, locals at her pub fondly remembered that she still "owed a slate at the bar" (personal correspondence from Ben Levy to Author).

Betty May's later letters reveal just how lonely she was feeling at this time and how she was mindful and reflective about how she was physically ageing and also that her pace of life had slowed down immensely. Some of what she said to Garnett included: "time flies and I have been in the flat for nine years nearly," and that she "lives a pretty placid existence ... there comes a time in life when one has to slow down, which I am certainly doing" (Northwestern University, Special Collections/Letters). This is astrologically pertinent to Betty May as, at the time of her death, transiting Pluto was conjunct her natal Saturn in the fourth house (the area of home and family life), and both Saturn and Pluto are associated with cycles of beginnings and endings, physically and metaphorically speaking.

This transit between Pluto and Saturn indicates that there would be inevitable transformations in her life at that time, and even psychological changes too. Even after considerable difficulties, she would still have to expect great changes. This was certainly borne out, for not only did her partner Billy die, but she was left financially insecure. This included her debts, as well as having to move home some years after he had died. At the time that she died, her progressed Sun was in Scorpio (the sign ruled by Pluto). This is pertinent as Pluto is associated with death and transformation, as previously discussed. Its energy is deeply intense too so she may have been feeling more emotional than usual and realised that her earthly life was not for much longer. She was feeling vulnerable too about her ill-health and disclosed to Garnett previously that "since my accident, I have been unable to go out quite so much," she didn't however say what the accident was, possibly it was a fall. She also wrote and informed him that she had "been getting rather giddy feelings, and I don't go out except to pay my rent every Monday morning" (ibid). She also tells Garnett in her letter that her friend, Iris, does her weekend shopping for her. She continued that every Sunday, Pat, the lady who Billy fell in love with, comes to see how she is (ibid). Perhaps Pat felt guilty about her affair with Billy Barfoot and somehow felt that she owed something to Betty May after he died.

The written communication between her and Garnett continued and in April, 1977, three years before she died, she wrote to him once again. This time she was asking him for money saying that "things are terribly expensive here" (ibid). In that same letter she recognises his consistent kindness to her over a long period of time: "you are the very last person who I should come to for help because you have been so very kind to me all these years" (ibid). Perhaps she had to ask him as he was the *only* person she could ask, and she may have felt too proud to ask her friends Iris or Pat, or she may have known that they could not afford to lend her the money. At least there was the National Health Service to support her as well as Social Security, now called the Department of Work & Pensions (or D.W.P.), which did not exist when she was a child and younger woman.

Betty May died in May of 1980 and she did not have a next of kin to report the death to, so a member of staff from the hospital was responsible for registering her death. That person from Chatham Hospital recalled Betty May vividly some 42 years later, which shows her nothing had changed in terms of her distinctive and unique personality, even when she was in her eighties. Betty May said to the hospital staff member in her last days that in her lifetime she "had received enough morphine to kill a horse" (personal correspondence to Author). This is typical of the jovial and witty, perhaps even exaggerated comments that Betty May would have spoken. Astrologically, it not only pertains to the Sun sextile Jupiter aspect in her natal chart, but on the day she died, transiting Jupiter was also conjunct her Sun. This showed that her life of excess had taken its toll on her health and her life had come to an end. Transiting Saturn was also conjunct Chiron in Virgo when she died. This indicates that she had come to rely on the authorities, and that reality had finally caught up with her. Previously, she had relied on the security and support of friends and lovers. However, now that she was at a mature age and many of her peers had died, she respected what the local authorities could offer her in terms of council housing, social care, as well as the National Health Service.

Photograph by Kind Permission of Fanny Garnett

Bessie Golding died at a very young age, metaphorically speaking, when she created Betty May, in order that she could live the life that she wanted in the best way she knew how. She survived the two World Wars and the Spanish Flu pandemic, which shows her strength and ability to be at the right place at the right time in terms of avoiding ailments and an early death. Also relevant to her, she saw The Witchcraft Act repealed in 1951 and replaced by the Fraudulent Mediums Act (which in turn was repealed in 2008). It was some 70 years previous to Betty May's birth that, in 1824, Parliament passed The Vagrancy Act. Under this law, astrology, fortune-telling and spiritualism became punishable offences; the repeal of The Witchcraft Act was progress of sorts for practitioners of these divinatory arts.

She also lived through a period where education and employment rights were eventually granted for females, and where women of different classes were eventually given the vote. Despite these advancements, she remained in a society (right up until her death) where classism, ageism, racism and sexism remained. Throughout her life, she was somewhat independent. For example, behaving just as she pleased, which often went against the grain of what society expected from a woman – yet, at the same time she remained fiercely dependent on others for her financial security, particularly after her modelling career finished (as noted earlier).

Betty May was proud of her artistic achievements and often boasted to others about the celebrities she had met, as well as the artists she befriended and sat for. As we know, she was also notorious and came under the spotlight in court cases and tabloid newspapers, especially in the mid to late 1930's, when by this time she was in her forties. It is understandable that she was proud of her modelling; for in daring to dream and romanticise about a life that contrasted with her family (and the previous Golding and James generations), she was able to escape from the harsh squalor and turmoil of the environment that she knew of the East End of London.

BETTY MAY (1894-1980)

ACKNOWLEDGEMENTS, CREDITS & REFERENCES

Rodden classification rating of rectified natal chart – 'X'.

Bessie Golding rectified natal chart – 1:00am, 25/08/1894, West Ham, 0e01,51n31.

My special thanks to:

- Fanny Garnett, the sole surviving daughter of David Garnett, who graciously permitted me to use the photograph of Betty May when she was a pensioner living in Kent, which is held by the McCormick Library of Special Collections & University Archives, Northwestern University, Evanston, IL.
- Julian Bell for communication to Fanny Garnett for me, regarding the photograph of the older Betty May Sedgwick.

I am also thankful to the following people, whose assistance, generosity of spirit and sharing of information have been invaluable to this piece of research and writing:

- Ian Black – With particular thanks, for his kindness and patience. His passion for accuracy, detail and analysis re: the family genealogy website and the varying documents that accompany it and the historical context, this was invaluable to me. I am also grateful for his time in networking with various contacts of this project, especially the late and gracious Eleanore Atkins and her late grandson.
- Huge thanks to Mike Green historian and researcher. Thanks for humour and interest along the way and so many other areas connected with this project. Your shared knowledge of bohemians and their club scenes, also rare bohemian books as well as other journals and magazines, proof-reading, your knowledge of the East London and Essex in Betty May's early years, and for sharing various documents from the genealogy website –apologies for anything else I have forgotten here.
- Celine Hispiche, writer, performer and producer – for sharing her experience of performing and researching Betty May, as well as her generosity of spirit and overall exuberance and warmth.

- Benjamin Levy, artist, author and art-researcher – for his enthusiasm, kindness and shared integral information about Betty May.
- Wirksworth Heritage Centre – for confirmation through the 1939 Register of Betty May and Hubert Barfoot posing as 'Mr and Mrs Bailey'.

Further thanks are extended to the following people for sharing their wonderful memories and stories of Betty May Sedg(e)wick when she lived in Chatham and Rochester, Kent, in her later years:

- The late Eleonore Atkins for her memories and stories of Betty May Sedg(e)wick in her later years, when she was her 'home-help'.
- Bernard Cherry for his memories of when he drank with his peers in The Queen Charlotte pub in Kent, and his recollections of Betty May holding court with his group of friends.
- Jane Dalley for her loving and warm memories of conversations that Betty May had with her and her family in The Man of Kent pub in Rochester, Kent.
- Anonymous – for the memories of Betty May when she was in Chatham Hospital for her final days.

And last but not least:

- Steve at 100th Monkey Press – for information regarding Bobby Barfoot in Crowley's diaries, as well as sharing texts from Leah Hirsch and Raoul Loveday.
- Glenn Mitchell, inquisitive bookseller of *Peter Harrington Books* – for help with the pricing of different editions of *Tiger Woman, My Story*, and also proof-reading.
- The London Society of Art-Dealers administrator – for checking their membership records from the 1930's.
- McCormick Library of Special Collections & University Archives, Northwestern University, Evanston, IL. – for access to the letters of Betty May to David Garnett from the early 1960's to the late 1970's: MS164, Box 50, Folder 10.

- The Metropolitan Police Service Heritage Centre (Curatorial Services) – for information on Robert George Golding's duration in the police force, his warrant number, along with register of leaving date and locations covered during service.
- Dr Philip Young, Assistant Librarian at The Warburg Institute, School of Advanced Study, University of London – for accessing the photograph of Betty May in a jumper (dated approx. 1923) and for permitting the photograph to be published.
- Thanks to the archivist at Kent History and Library Centre, for searching various pieces of information pertaining to Betty May/Sedgwick
- Thanks to the Medway Archives for searching various pieces of information pertaining to Betty May/Sedgwick

CERTIFICATES

Birth:

Bessie Golding: 25th August, 1894, Canning Town, County of West Ham. Vol 04a, page 114.

Marriages:

Miles Linzee Atkinson to Betty Marlow Golding, 9th September, 1914, St. Marylebone. Vol. 01a, page 1623.

George Dibbs King Waldron to Betty Marlow Atkinson, 4th November, 1916, Henrietta St. Registry Office, London. Vol. 01a, page 1268.

Frederick Charles Loveday to Betty May Golding, 3rd September, 1922, Oxford. Vol. 3a, page 2930.

Noel Mostyn Sedgwick to Betty May Loveday, 26th February, 1926, St. Pancras. Vol. 01b, page 178.

Death:

Hubert William Barfoot: 2nd January, 1963, All Saints Hospital, Chatham, Kent. Vol. 05b, page 479 (address: 248 High St., Rochester).

Betty May Sedg(e)wick: 5th May, 1980, Medway Hospital, Gillingham, Kent. Vol 16, page 630.

George Golding: 20th February, 1915, Temporary Military Hospital, Salisbury, Wiltshire. Vol. 05a, page 288.

Thanks to:

Central Family Court, High Holborn, London, WC1V 6NP – for copy of divorce papers between Miles Linzee Atkinson and Betty May.

Principle Registry of the Family Division of the High Court of Justice – for copy of the certificate of making Decree Nisi Absolute (divorce) Atkinson and Betty May.

National Archives – for divorce papers of Betty May Waldron and George Dibbs King Waldron and co-respondent Leonard E. Van Leer. Ref No. at National Archives: J77/1490/6030.

The London Metropolitan Archives – for admission & discharge record for Bessie Golding from St. George in the East Workhouse Infirmary (Tower Hamlets & Stepney), 15th June, 1912. Ref. No. STBG/SG/118/88. Old Gravel Lane Infirmary, Master of the Workhouse J.R. Moloney. T.J. Edwards (Steward) Michalmas, September, 1912 – Bessie Golding discharged from Infirmary. Ref. No. (ibid). Also for school registers for the London Borough of Tower Hamlets: LCC & ILEA School Admission & Registers for Bessie Golding (Betty May) and George Golding (her brother).

Agnes Hart's pension card courtesy of **The Ministry of Pensions and National Insurance.** Card/O.A.F. 262309/OA.1166.

Northwestern University, IL, U.S.A. – Charles Deering McCormick, Library of Special Collections – for letters to David Garnett from Betty May. Ref: MS164 – box file 50.

BOOKS

Avery, S. (1982) *The Rising Sign – Your Astrological Mask*. Doubleday.

Avery, S. and Graham, Katherine M. **(Editor) (2018)** *Sex, Time and Place – Queer Histories of London c.1850 to the Present*. Bloomsbury Academic.

Bakewell, B. (1999) *Fitzrovia: London's Bohemia*. National Portrait Gallery Publications.

Basu, A. (2019) *Fitzrovia: The Other Side of Oxford Street – A Social History 1900–1950*. The History Press.

Churton, T. (2021) *Aleister Crowley in England – The Return of the Great Beast*. Inner Traditions.

David, H. (1988) *The Fitzrovians: A Portrait of Bohemian Society 1900-1955*. Michael Joseph.

Deghy G. and K. Waterhouse. (1955) *Café Royal – Ninety Years of Bohemia*. Hutchison & Co. (Publishers) Ltd.

Fiber, S. (2014) *The Fitzroy – The Autobiography of a London Tavern*. Sally Fiber in conjunction with DeSapinaud.

(Edited by) Frewin, L. and (Foreword by) Greene, G. (1963) *The Café Royal Story*. London: Hutchison Benham.

Garnett, D. (1955) *The Flowers of the Forest*. Chatto & Windus, London.

Hamnett, N. (1984) *The Laughing Torso*. Virago Press Limited.

Hill, L. (2004) *360 Degrees of Wisdom – Charting Your Destiny with the Sabian Oracle*. Plume.

Hobday, C. (1989) *Edgell Rickword – A Poet at War*. Carcanet Press Limited.

Holroyd, M. (1996) *Augustus John – The New Biography*. Chatto and Windas, London.

Hooker, D. (1986) *Nina Hamnett: Queen of Bohemia*. Constable and Co. Limited.

Johnson, J. and Greutzner, A. (1986) *The Dictionary of British Artists 1880-1940*. Antique Collectors' Club.

Kaczynski, R. (2010) *Perdurabo – The Life of Aleister Crowley*. North Atlantic Books.

Kaldera, R. (2011) *Moon Phase Astrology*. Destiny Books.

Knights, S. (2015) *A Life of David Garnett – Bloomsbury's Outsider*. Bloomsbury Reader.

Kohn, M. (2001) *Dope Girls – The Birth of the British Drug Underground*. Grata Books.

Lindsay, J. (1962) *Fanfrolico and After*. The Bodley Head Ltd.

Marshall-Calder, A. (1990) *The Magic of my Youth*. Cardinal in Sphere Books Ltd.

May, B. (2014) *Tiger Woman, My Story – The Incredible Life that Inspired the New Musical 'Betty May'*. Published by Duckworth Overlook.

Michaud, J. and Hilverson, K. (1993) *The Saturn Pluto Phenomenon*. Samuel Weiser, Inc.

Nevinson, C.R.W. RBA RO1 NEAC (1938) *Paint and Prejudice (with 32 illustrations from the author's work)*. Published by Harcourt, Brace & Co., New York.

Nicholson, V. (2003) *Among the Bohemians – Experiments in Living 1900-1939*. Penguin Books Ltd.

Pentelow, M. and Rowe, M. (2001) *Characters of Fitzrovia*. Chatto & Windus in association with Felix Dennis.

Peterson Merello, L. (2018) *The Women Who Inspired London Art – The Avico Sisters and Other Models of the Early 20th Century*. Pen & Sword Books Ltd.

Reinhart, M. (1989) *Chiron and the Healing Journey – An Astrological and Psychological Perspective*. Penguin Books Ltd.

Renninson, N. (2017) *Bohemian London – From Pre-Raphaelites to Punk*. Oldcastle Books.

Rickword, E. (1976) *Behind the Eyes*. Carcanet New Press Limited in association with Carcanet Press Limited.

River, L. and Gillespie, S. (1987) *The Knot of Time – Astrology and the Female Experience*. The Women's Press Limited.

Spurling, H. (2017) *Anthony Powell*. Hamish Hailton.

(Edited by) Symonds, J. and Grant, K. (1979) *The Confessions of Aleister Crowley – An Autohagiography*.

E-BOOKS

Epstein, J. (2014) *Let there be Sculpture*. Kindle Edition.

NEWSPAPER ARTICLES

https://www.britishnewspaperarchive.co.uk/ – *Truth* newspaper, Wed. 19th June, 1929, advert on p41: 'Betty May -TICEIR (*sic*)

WOMAN, Epstein's famous model speaks out in this amazing autobiograpy' (sic). Tiger Woman My Story.

The Daily Express, 06/02/1918: 'Epstein Model in Prison, Embarrassing End To A Trip To France.'

The Evansville Courier, Evansville, Indiana: 'The Angel Child Who "Saw Hell" and Came Back' by W.B. Seabrook, 19th August, 1928, p37.

The Daily Mirror: 'As I See It' and 'Models Become Cooks', 20th June, 1929.

Folkestone, Hythe, Sandgate & Cheriton Herald, Saturday 30th May, 1942, p7.

Pittsburgh Sunday Telegraph, Sunday February 16th, 1930: 'By Dolores, The Fatal Woman of the London Studios' (page number unknown).

The Police Gazette (from the British Newspaper Archives), 28th January, 1916: article about Harry Melford aka Hyman Coutts having a conviction for importuning male persons for immoral practices (page number unknown).

PHOTOGRAPHS

Thanks to:

The Liverpool Echo – for granting permission to use the black and white photograph of Betty May in her coat and hat when she appeared at The Old Bailey in April, 1934.

The National Library of Scotland – for the image of the map showing Lansdowne and Portland Road in Canning Town, reproduced with the permission of the National Library of Scotland, Creative Commons CC – by-4.0.

The Northwestern University, IL. – for assistance with the file of letters from Betty May to David Garnett and the advice regarding the photograph of Betty May as a senior citizen.

The University of Sydney, Australia (www.heuristplus.sydney.edu.au) – the source for the photo of George Dibbs Kings Waldron.

WEBSITES

https://www.angelfire.com/ga3/thelema/crowley/un1934b.htm – Accessed in 2020,-source unknown, April 1934 – The Trial of Aleister Crowley.

https://archiveshub.jisc.ac.uk/searc/archives/41462b79-627c-3d7c-bdfa-76ab961598c1 – Accessed on 07/10/2020-Duckworths publishers.

http://www.elisarolle.com/queerplaces/pqrst/Raoul%20Loveday.html – Accessed on 19/02/2022. Betty May in 1914 disliking Aleister Crowley. – Accessed on 22/02/2022. Dibbs King Waldron divorced Betty May because of her drug dependency.

https://en.wikipedia.org/wiki/Betty_May#cite_ref-94 – Accessed on 19/12/2020. Letter put out by Duckworth's trying to find Betty May and the Daily Express story that she had been found.

https://fashionista.com/2017/04/bob-short-haircut-hairstyle-history – Accessed on 03/02/2022. History of the 'bob' haircut.

https://fomphc.com/heritage-centre/ – Accessed on 10/11/2020. Detail of police officer Robert George Golding.

www.guttedarcades.blogspot.com/2012/07/betty-may-html – Accessed on 16/10/2020. A quote about witchy appearance and also information about Betty May and Gabriel and Malcolm Lowry.

http://www.imagekind.com/MemberProfile.aspx?MID=5222a48c-2b67-4f63-9d88-56e4ce35db1e – Accessed on 01/02/2022. Angus Basil, a pacifist.

www.londonmetropolitanarchives.com – Accessed on 12/01/2021. Information about admission to the Raine Street Workhouse and the discharge into the Infirmary and duration there.

www.nationalarchives.gov.uk – Accessed 2021. Shipping Record for Betty May Loveday travelling to America from Southampton on the 'SS America'.

https://navigator.health.org.uk/theme/dangerous-drugs-act-1920-criminalising-opium-and-cocaine-possession – Accessed on 13/11/2021. Information on the introduction of the Dangerous Drugs Acts of 1920 and 1928.

https://pasttenseblog.wordpress.com/2020/07/22/today-in-londons-striking-herstory-1890-sweet-victory-east-end-chocolate-factory-workers-win-strike/ – Accessed on 04/02/2022. Chocolate factories in the East End.

https://www.rambert.org.uk/performance-database/works/lady-into-fox-wrk103/ – Accessed on 02/11/2021. 'Lady into Fox' novel performed at the Mercury Theatre in London.

www.royaldocks.london/articles/a-history-of-the-royal-docks – Accessed on 08/11/2020. A thriving cargo industry.

https://scblog.lib.byu.edu/2017/08/04/the-victorian-shilling-shocker/ – Accessed on 27/01/2022.

stgitehistory.org.uk/media/ratcliffhighway.html – Accessed on 30/12/2020. 'Tigresses' name given to feisty prostitutes.

www.thetimes.co.uk/archives – Accessed on 11/02/2021. Mrs Sedgwick's former life, drink, drugs and immortality.

www.wiki.casebook.org/rose_mylett.html – Accessed on 03/04/2021. Story of Robert Golding finding Rose Mylett's dead body.

https://en.wikipedia.org/wiki/Crab_Tree_Club – Accessed on 20/02/2022. Paul Nash commenting on The Crab Tree Club.

www.100thmonkeypress.com. Diary entries of Aleister Crowley for Bobby Barfoot and Raoul Loveday (circa 03/12/1922) on his first week at the Abbey of Thelema. Also Leah Hirsig, February 12th, 1923, on the violent scene that Betty May created.

Glossary of Terms

Ascendant: The sign of the zodiac ascending at the time of one's birth on the eastern horizon, it is also known as the 'rising sign'.

Aspect: An angle the planets make to each other in the horoscope, as well as with the Ascendant, Midheaven, Descendant and Lower Heaven (IC). A **hard aspect** refers to major angles created between planets, which comprise of the conjunction, opposition and square angles (n.b. the conjunction is variable, depending on the energies of the two planets involved). **Sextile** is a soft aspect which creates an angle at 60 degrees with another planet. **Trine** is a soft aspect which creates a 120 degree angle with another planet.

Aspect patterns: Involves three or more planets making a configuration in different ways. There are several of them and examples are: the T-Square, Grand Trine, Yod, Grand Cross and Kite.

Benefic: A benefic (beneficiary) planet is one which bestows positive energies which can, for example, provide constructiveness and support.

Chiron: An asteroid that in astrology symbolises the 'Wounded Healer' – it represents our deepest wounds and endeavours to heal them. Chiron orbits the Sun between Saturn and Uranus.

Detriment: A planet which is positioned in the zodiac sign opposite the sign it rules.

Ecliptical: The ecliptical is the great circle that is the apparent path of the Sun among the constellations in the course of a year. The constellations of the zodiac are arranged along the ecliptic.

Exaltation: Each of the seven traditional planets has its exaltation in one zodiac sign; the Sun in Aries, the Moon in Taurus, Mercury in Virgo, Venus in Pisces, Mars in Capricorn, Jupiter in Cancer and Saturn in Libra.

Fall: A planet is said to be in fall when it is in the sign opposite the one it is exalted in. When a planet is in fall it is thought to be debilitated in that sign. For example, the Sun is exalted in Aries and so is in fall in Libra.

Imum Coeli/IC: Latin for 'bottom of the sky'. The Imum Coeli is the 'nadir' or low point in the Sun's path and, if you could see the Sun, where it would be seen at midnight. It is also the cusp of the fourth house.

Midheaven /MC Coeli: Latin for 'heaven', the Medium Coeli is the Midheaven, where the Sun would be at noon, at the top of the chart. It is also the tenth house cusp.

Modes: There are three modes in astrology which are represented by cardinal, fixed and mutable energies. They all represent the way in which a sign operates. **Cardinal** signs are initiators of action and are the signs of Aries, Cancer, Libra and Capricorn. **Fixed** signs have staying power and are the signs of Taurus, Leo, Scorpio and Aquarius. **Mutable** signs have a versatile attitude and are the signs of Gemini, Virgo, Sagittarius and Pisces.

Natal chart: A picture of the positions of the signs, planets and angles at the time of one's birth. It contains data such as date, time and place of birth – to generate an accurate astrological chart.

Natural zodiac: A system whereby the twelve signs of the zodiac are assigned to the twelve houses in the birth chart, given that they have similar characteristics. For example, the first sign, Aries, is associated with the first house, them both being about the self; the second sign, Taurus, is associated with the second house, given that Taurus is about possessions and the second house is about resources; and so on.

Polarity: There are six polarities in astrology which are natural oppositions. They comprise of Aries/Libra, Taurus/Scorpio, Gemini/Sagittarius, Cancer/Capricorn, Leo/Aquarius and Virgo/Pisces. The signs are also male and female – the air and fire are masculine and the earth and water feminine.

Retrograde: This is when a planet appears to be moving backwards against the backdrop of the stars.

Rodden Rating System: A system developed by astrologer, Lois Rodden, which classifies astrological data by grade to reflect its accuracy for research and purposes for astrologers. Classification

GLOSSARY OF TERMS

starts at 'AA' then 'A' and finishes at 'XX' – for further details, see https://www.astro.com/astro-databank/Help:RR.

Rose Cross: A symbol largely associated with the founder of the Rosicrucian Order. It symbolises the teachings of a Western esoteric tradition with Christian principles. The rose is either gold, red or white.

Sabian Symbols: A system of 360 unique images pertaining to each degree of the zodiac, developed in 1925 by Marc Edmund Jones and Elsie Wheeler. The degree in the natal chart needs to be rounded up to the next degree in order to obtain the correct number for the Sabian Symbol of that sign, e.g. the Sun 26 degrees Pisces is rounded up to 27 degrees, and then the Sabian Symbol for 27 degrees Pisces has to be read for the interpretation.

Tarot: A Tarot deck consists of 78 cards; divided into the Major Arcana of 22 cards and the Minor Arcana of 56 cards, which are divided into four suits of Wands, Coins or Pentacles, Swords and Cups. The Minor Arcana cards correspond to the four elements; Wands – fire, Coins or Pentacles – earth, Swords – air and Cups – water. A Tarot deck can be used for divination and spiritual advice and self-development.

Thelema: A set of magical, mystical and religious beliefs formed by Aleister Crowley in the twentieth century. The Law of Thelema is: 'Do What Thou Wilt Shall Be The Whole Of The Law' and means: to live by one's own true will (hence: 'what thou wilt').

Traditional astrology: This was the type of astrology which was practiced up until the seventeenth century, before the arrival of The Age of Reason (aka The Scientific Age). Traditional Astrology focused on answering a specific question at a specific time using the traditional planets; the Sun, the Moon, Mercury, Venus, Mars, Jupiter, and Saturn.

T-Square: A pattern formed when planets in opposition also form a square with another planet. The pattern resembles the letter 'T' when viewed in the chart. The squared planet or point is referred to as the 'release point'. T-Squares are made of up of each of the modes; cardinal, fixed and mutable.

www.ingramcontent.com/pod-product-compliance
Lightning Source LLC
Chambersburg PA
CBHW061758110426
42742CB00012BB/2044